# SharePoint
## for
# Nonprofits

## The Definitive Guide to SharePoint for your Nonprofit, Association, Charity and .ORG

# John Stover • Sean Bordner

# SharePoint for Nonprofits

The Definitive SharePoint Guide for your Nonprofit, Association, Charity and .ORG

## By John Stover and Sean Bordner

Edited by Josh Bordner

Contact John Stover at John.Stover@gmail.com
Contact Sean Bordner at Sean.Bordner@gmail.com

Printed in the United States of America
First Printing: November 2010
ISBN-13 978-0-557-85140-9

*For my wife, Kathleen, who made this possible with her support, encouragement and tolerance for my constant rambling about SharePoint. I'd like to thank my coworkers, clients, colleagues, my parents, and especially my children, Emma, Faith, and Jack, for giving me so many opportunities to learn. Thank you.*

*John*

*This would not have been possible without my wife, Misty, who's love and companionship I cherish more than the air I breathe - those around me in both my professional life and my personal voyage have enriched me - I am surrounded by an enormous amount of talent which encourages thought and growth - my dear friends and beloved family and children, Parker, Kyle and Ava. Thank you.*

*Sean*

**John Stover** is a consultant, solution architect, instructor and Microsoft technology specialist. He is an expert in web content management, ecommerce, social networking, governance, information architecture, and project management. John presents frequently at conferences, seminars, user groups, and workshops. His expertise and passion for technology is present in his presentations and his writing. John has had the opportunity to work for various organizations from Fortune 100 companies to Federal Government agencies, and he is particularly passionate about associations and nonprofits. As an architect and consultant, he focuses on enhancing and mobilizing membership and volunteer-based initiatives and organizations. He is PMP certified and has multiple Microsoft certifications including MCT and MCTS. John lives at Lake Holiday in Virginia with his wife, Kathleen, and their children Emma, Faith and Jack.

**Email**: John.Stover@gmail.com

**Sean Bordner** is a SharePoint Solution Architect who has worked extensively with associations and nonprofits through the past decade. He has a technical background with past positions ranging from Sr. Programmer and Technical Manager to Sr. Solution Architect and Engineer. His specific areas of expertise include public websites (WCM), community sites, SharePoint and FAST Search, search engine optimization (SEO), information architecture (site structure and taxonomy), SharePoint governance and best practices related to planning, architecting, and deploying high visibility SharePoint solutions. He holds many Microsoft certifications; including MCT, MCTS, MCSD, MCP, MCAD. He is a Microsoft Certified Trainer who excels at communicating sophisticated concepts in an easy-to-understand and usable format. He serves as the Community Manager for the largest SharePoint Group on LinkedIn. He also serves as the Community Manager for TheSUG.org, a global SharePoint User Group community.

**Email**: Sean.Bordner@gmail.com

# At a Glance

# Table of Contents

# Table of Contents

# Table of Contents

# Preface

## Why Did We Write This Book?

We wrote this book to get famous. The millions of dollars that we're going to receive from book sales will be nice, but we really want the adoring fans. It's pretty clear that anyone who writes a book gains instant fame and fortune, especially if the book is about an exciting technology topic. We've even been working on some ideas about who should be cast when this is made into a movie. Yeah. We want that.

We also wrote this book for you. We want you to understand how SharePoint can benefit your organization. We have been educating people for years on how to use SharePoint, and we have been asked the same questions over and over.

There are already hundreds of books in print about SharePoint. As of this writing, there are 936 books available from Amazon on SharePoint.

**Books** > "sharepoint"

**Related Searches:** sharepoint 2007, sharepoint 2010, sharepoint development.

Showing 1 - 12 of 936 Results

**Amazon.com Search Results for "SharePoint" Books**

Nearly all of those books are written for administrators and developers. This book is different. This book will not teach you how to write code or how to install SharePoint. This book does provide an introduction to SharePoint. This book will give you an idea how organizations are using SharePoint today and what can be accomplished with it. We hope to provide the knowledge you need to implement SharePoint as a successful business productivity platform.

We've worked with organizations of all sizes. We've worked with nonprofits and associations with more than 50 million members. We've also worked with the smallest of charities. Between the two of us, we've worked with hundreds of different organizations using SharePoint.

We've worked with Fortune 500 companies, small private companies, government agencies from local to federal, and schools of all kinds. We have learned a tremendous amount about how different types of organizations function. We've learned even more about how to make SharePoint work for you.

There are a lot of people using SharePoint. No, really. A lot of people. According to Microsoft, there are millions of licensed SharePoint users. Combine that with all of the public-facing websites and there really are hundreds of millions of SharePoint users.

Even with so many users, there are comparatively few people who really understand SharePoint. People know how to use it to store files, but they don't understand how to leverage it to enhance their organization. They know it can store content; they just don't know how well it can manage information, enable communication, foster collaboration, turn data into information, and provide knowledge.

It's odd considering the broad adoption of SharePoint. SharePoint really is everywhere.

SharePoint is being used in small, localized groups of just a few people and in the largest of government organizations here and abroad. If SharePoint is so flexible and used so pervasively throughout the world, why is it still so misunderstood?

We wrote this book to help you gain a better understanding of SharePoint. What is it? What is it capable of? How can you benefit from it?

We made our lives easier writing this book by using the word "org" to represent a variety of organizations: nonprofit, not-for-profit, charity, charitable organization, non-governmental organization (NGO); and associations of all types, including trade, volunteer, social, and community. An org is different than a traditional business or government agency. Orgs behave differently. Orgs are structured differently. Simply said, orgs are different.

Many of these differences provide challenges unique to an org, but many of these same differences provide great opportunities. Orgs are staff, members, volunteers, and donors. Orgs are products, conferences, dues, chapters, commerce, content, government affairs, lobbying, legal, publications, marketing, education, communication, and community. Orgs are passionate. Orgs make a difference. Orgs are different.

## Who should read this book?

This book is for professionals who work with nonprofits, associations, and orgs of all kinds. Executives, technical staff, business users, managers, senior professionals, and junior staff members can all learn something from this book. If you are a community leader, an education manager, an association member, or even a volunteer, this book is for you. We've shared a lot of SharePoint information as well as many org-specific ideas and concepts.

SharePoint has an enormous amount of capability. We wrote this book to introduce you to the breadth and depth of SharePoint and to be your road map for evaluating and implementing SharePoint with your org.

## What is SharePoint?

SharePoint is a product. No wait, SharePoint is a toolkit. No, that's still not right. SharePoint is a platform.

You've probably heard a lot of rumors about SharePoint. Some of the rumors may be true, but some of the rumors are definitely myths. In order to clear the air, we need to start with a very basic question. What is SharePoint?

**SharePoint is software used to build web sites.**

If you cut through all of the marketing hype, that's what it is. SharePoint is software used to build websites. How's that for an opaque answer?

Microsoft®
# SharePoint· Server 2010

SharePoint can be used to build all types of websites, from private websites for your staff or members to public-facing websites for the world to see. SharePoint can be used off the shelf. You can also customize every single aspect of SharePoint to make it exactly what you need.

SharePoint is a set of Microsoft products and technologies which are used to build websites. To geek out a bit, SharePoint runs on Windows Server, SQL Server, and IIS (the web server that ships with Windows Server). SharePoint is a .NET application, built with .NET, and can be extended with .NET. SharePoint has a complete and fully documented application programming interface (API) and a web services interface. SharePoint has a software development kit (SDK) available complete with sample code.

SharePoint is bigger than just Microsoft. SharePoint has an entire ecosystem of companies that have third-party add-ons, management utilities, Web Parts, widgets, and solutions available. There are hundreds of books, thousands of blog posts, and countless online discussions about SharePoint. There is even an open source community for sharing free code and solutions for SharePoint.

Now, if you mix all of that together and run it through a strainer, what does it really mean? SharePoint is software used to build web sites.

We're not going to give you a history lesson on SharePoint. You don't need it. Just realize that SharePoint has been around for more than a decade. Microsoft started working on what would become SharePoint in the late 1990's for its first public release in 2001. SharePoint is now in its fourth major release, SharePoint 2010.

This is not a niche piece of software written by some kids working out of their mother's basement. This is an enterprise business productivity platform architected, developed, and supported by the *largest* software company in the world. With a little bit of education,

SharePoint is one of the most intuitive and easy-to-use website solutions available anywhere.

SharePoint can enable efficiencies across your org, inside and out. You can save time *and* money. You will have an increase in productivity. You can standardize documents, templates, and business processes. You can standardize applications and even your application platform. Standardize your global taxonomy, user experience, and software management. You can standardize. Period.

SharePoint is a single platform that is useful across your entire org. This is important and worth repeating. You can leverage *a single platform* across your entire org. One technology platform that is useful for all of your supporters – staff, members, donors, volunteers, board members, affiliates, partners, and the public. Concentrate on what you need to do and spend less time supporting a disparate set of technologies and applications.

Welcome to SharePoint.

# SharePoint Versions: Three Card Monte

The word *SharePoint* is actually a generic term for a collection of products. Within this umbrella term of SharePoint are a variety of technologies and even different versions of SharePoint. We'll cover these in more detail later, but here are the big three: SharePoint Foundation 2010, SharePoint Server 2010 Standard, and SharePoint Server 2010 Enterprise.

## SharePoint Foundation 2010

SharePoint Foundation 2010, or just SharePoint Foundation, is server software that provides the baseline "foundation" capabilities of SharePoint. SharePoint Foundation is free with Windows Server. That's right – it's free. Your org can take advantage of SharePoint Foundation when you are licensed to use Windows Server 2008 at no cost.

Everything in SharePoint Foundation is also in the other two versions of SharePoint: Ribbon Toolbar, Accessibility, Mobile Connectivity, Cross-Browser Support, Microsoft Office client integration, Search, and a lot more.

SharePoint Foundation lets you build websites easily using nothing but your web browser. You can build websites using Sites, Pages, Lists, Libraries, Alerts, Web Parts, and Workflows.

You can build one website, or you can build a thousand websites. These websites could be isolated and independent, or nested in a logical hierarchical structure. SharePoint Foundation websites can be brochure-ware or full collaboration websites. SharePoint Foundation has tools for Document Libraries, shared Calendars, Task Lists, Surveys, Discussion Boards, Picture Libraries, Custom Lists, and a lot more. You can use Workflows and Search. This free software is incredibly powerful.

SharePoint Foundation also has robust security. You determine who gets to use your SharePoint Sites. Either open it up or lock it down. A team can work together in one private Site with another team collaborating in a completely different private Site. Some individuals may even work in both Sites. Sites can be for staff only or can include members, volunteers, donors, and board members. Sites can also be public-facing websites and can allow anonymous users.

SharePoint Foundation provides a framework for authenticating users. Regardless of where you store and manage your user information, your org's user data can be used *as it exists today*.

SharePoint Foundation can leverage *your* Association Management System software (AMS), *your* Customer Relationship Management system (CRM), *your* homegrown database, or *your* Active Directory (AD). If an Excel file is where you keep a list of your members, SharePoint Foundation can even use that spreadsheet as the authoritative user authentication information. By the way, that's a horrible idea, but we know it happens. Trust us, we've seen it.

SharePoint Foundation can *easily* connect to external data with Business Connectivity Services. We really mean easily. You can wire SharePoint up to your external database and interact with the data in real time – **without writing any code.**

While SharePoint Foundation can interact with your existing data, it can also store data. SharePoint can be used to store contact lists, job listings, classifieds, member directories, vendor information, affiliates, a buyer's guide, and of course, documents. SharePoint Foundation can: capture form data; process applications; collect and manage abstract submissions; provide speaker management tools; and even update donor and volunteer information stored in your database.

Understand that SharePoint is designed to work *with* your org. You do not have to completely change everything about your org to work with SharePoint.

All of these capabilities are included in this FREE version of SharePoint. SharePoint Foundation is easy to download, install, and configure – literally less than 15 minutes and it's up and running. You can run everything needed for SharePoint Foundation on a single server or scale to a multiple-server farm for high availability. You can run SharePoint Foundation on virtual or physical servers. You can run SharePoint Foundation in your building, or run it in the cloud.

It's easy to understand, and it works great. You can work with SharePoint Foundation as soon as you install it, or you can configure and build robust applications.

At the other end of the spectrum is SharePoint Server 2010. SharePoint Server 2010 is not free. SharePoint Server 2010 is available in two versions: Standard and Enterprise. Both of these versions include all of the functionality of SharePoint Foundation 2010 and *many more*.

## SharePoint Server 2010 Standard

SharePoint Server 2010 Standard adds a lot of capabilities to the long list of features available in SharePoint Foundation. In fact, there are so many additional features that we could write a book dedicated to describing only the additions. We're trying to keep this very high level, so here are some highlights.

### Social

We have come to expect "Web 2.0" and "Social" features as part of our everyday collaborative lives. These features are just the latest of collaborative advancements which will continue to improve as ideas fuel technology. SharePoint makes it easier for people to work together. Everyone wants to work more efficiently and more effectively. We all work with other people; and working together is what it's all about. Collaboration has become quite a popular buzzword, and COLLABORATE literally means to work together.

Whether you call it Social Networking, Professional Networking, Web 2.0 or something else, SharePoint Server 2010 has social features baked in. Your users get robust social networking features that include My Profile, My Content, My Newsfeed, Ask Me About, Colleagues, Colleague Suggestions, Recent Activities, and Status Updates.

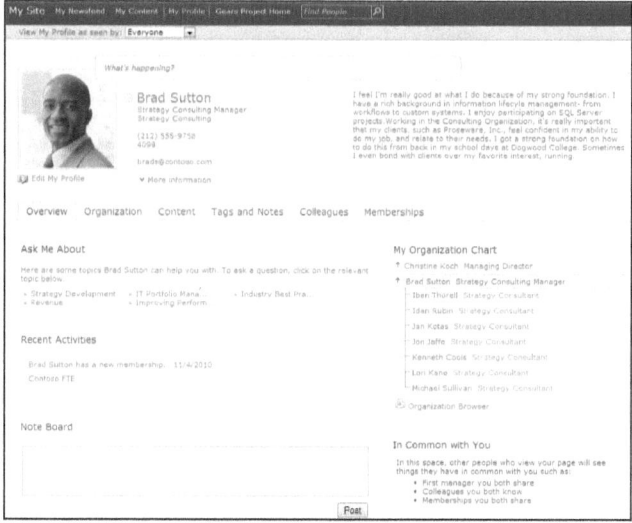

**SharePoint 2010 My Site**

With the social capabilities in SharePoint Server 2010, you can build your private social network for your org. By combining the inherent collaboration features with the social features, your social network can have segregated work areas which you can slice any way you wish.

Build groups based upon topic or interest. Construct specific areas for chapters, committees, councils, special interest groups, strategic groups, standards groups, or any other type of area needed in your org. Members can interact with staff. Staff can collaborate with volunteers. Donors, members, volunteers, trainers, staff, and even the general public can all collaborate, contribute, research, recommend, and socialize – TOGETHER.

## Web Content Management (WCM)

Microsoft calls it WCM. Most orgs call it CMS. SharePoint labels it Publishing. Whatever you call it; SharePoint has powerful and user-friendly tools for managing your website. While these capabilities exist within the SharePoint Server 2010 platform and can be used for your Intranet and extranet, SharePoint really shines when used for public-facing websites.

Your public-facing website has a lot of competition these days. It is no longer okay to simply have a web presence. Your website needs to be easily found from popular internet search engines like Google, Bing and Yahoo. It needs to retain the interest of a user who has, nowadays, the attention span of an average Kindergartener. Don't laugh; we're in the same category.

Your website needs to be organized logically and must contain fresh, relevant content. Users need to find whatever it is they are looking for quickly. Your website needs to work in all browsers, especially on mobile device.

On top of all that, your website needs to formally represent your org to the public – globally. Your org needs the tools to create, aggregate, prioritize, recommend, and deliver your messages.

SharePoint is, in fact, search engine friendly. With a proper implementation and a little SEO discipline, you will not have any problems with Google, Bing or Yahoo ranking your webpages high. Keeping the readers' attention is up to your content authors. Obviously, SharePoint can't help you write interesting things.

SharePoint does, however, make it easy to publish interesting content to your website. All too often the flow of fresh content gets bottlenecked at the IT level when they are busy keeping your infrastructure alive and safe (which is where their focus should be). Your authors can create and edit content directly on your SharePoint website. Their work can be reviewed and approved prior to going LIVE. The learning curve for your authors is virtually non-existent. If content authors are even remotely familiar with Microsoft Word, they will feel right at home in SharePoint.

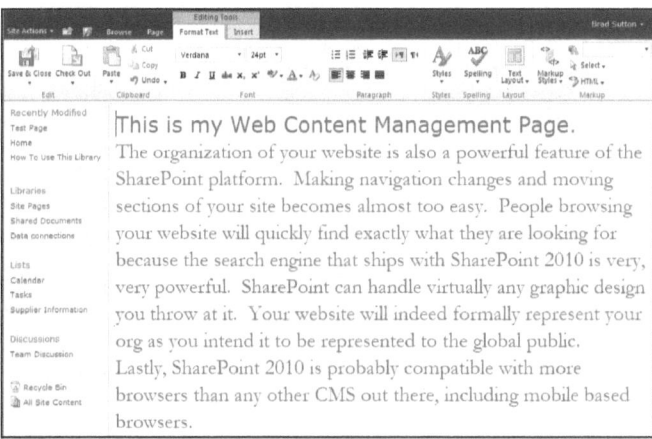

Page Editing in SharePoint 2010

Managing and organizing your website is easy with SharePoint. Making navigation changes and moving sections of your site becomes almost too easy. Your website users can quickly find exactly what they are looking for with the *extremely* powerful SharePoint Search. SharePoint can handle virtually any graphic design you throw at it. Your website will indeed formally represent your org as you intend it to be represented to the global public.

SharePoint 2010 is probably compatible with more browsers than any other CMS out there. They have learned hard lessons about compatibility issues. Remember Vista? Neither do we!

## Taxonomy

SharePoint Foundation provides a way for you to classify your content with single tiers of metadata using Columns. SharePoint Server 2010 adds advanced taxonomy and metadata capabilities. Driving this capability is the Managed Metadata Service – a centralized feature that lets you share a multi-faceted, multi-tiered, formal taxonomy structure across your entire org.

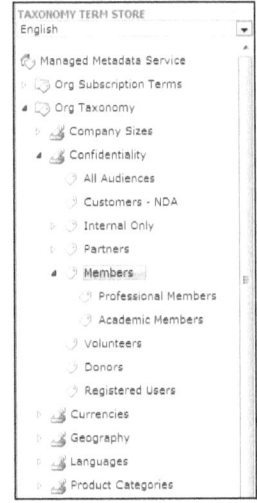

SharePoint Server provides features such as Keyword Suggestions, Metadata-driven Navigation, Tags, Notes, a Note Board, and Metadata-driven search refinements. Taxonomy is such an important topic that it merits a dedicated chapter.

**Manage Term Store**

## Advanced Content Management

SharePoint Foundation makes it easy to do basic content management using features like Document Libraries. For more robust Enterprise Content Management (ECM), SharePoint Server 2010 adds Document Sets, a Content Organizer, Multistage Disposition, Recently Authored Content, Unique Document IDs, and powerful Workflow Templates.

## Advanced Search Capabilities

Ask Me About, Best Bets, Basic Sorting, Federated Search, Click Through Relevancy, Duplicate Detection, Mobile Search Experience, Query Suggestions, "Did you mean?", Related Queries, and Search Scopes are all added as part of SharePoint 2010 Server. This is another topic we feel is important enough for a dedicated chapter.

# SharePoint Server 2010 Enterprise

SharePoint Server 2010 Enterprise is even bigger. Take everything available in SharePoint Foundation 2010 and add everything that ships with SharePoint Server 2010 Standard. Now add business intelligence (BI), reporting, and data integration tools. Then sprinkle in Office Services and *even more* Search enhancements, and we have SharePoint Server 2010 Enterprise.

## Excel Services

Excel Services lets you publish your Excel application to SharePoint. Your users can then see *and interact with* sheets, charts, pivot tables, pivot charts, and nearly any other application that you built in Excel. Users don't need Excel. They only need a browser. They can use a mobile device (iPhone, Blackberry, or Windows Mobile), a Mac, or a PC. Users can view and interact with your application built using Excel 2010.

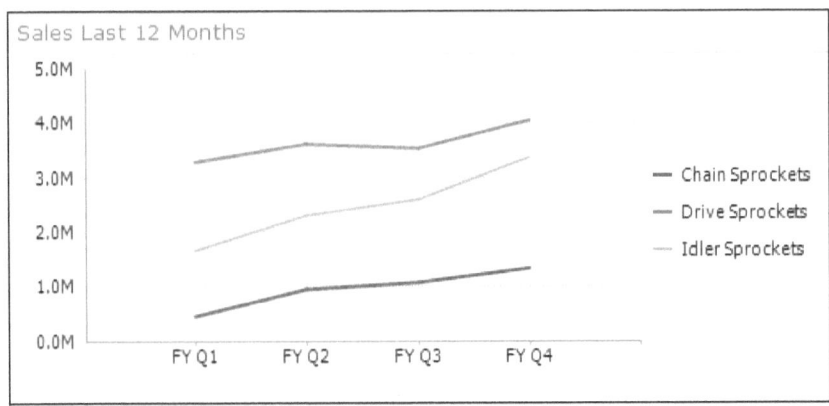

**Excel Services Web Part**

What makes this so cool? You already build applications in Excel. You're doing it today. Your CFO and CEO have built applications in Excel. We have seen entire applications constructed in Excel.

You do not have to redevelop that application in a different language using different tools. Publish your Excel application directly through SharePoint using Excel Services. Business users can build applications for SharePoint with the skills they have today.

## Visio Services

Did you know that Visio supports data integration? Have you ever seen a network architecture diagram made with Visio? Of course you have. Did you know you can use your network monitoring tools to feed the map you made with Visio? You can have a real visualization tool that lets you actually see on your network map which servers are up or down.

Visio Services lets you publish Visio 2010 diagrams to SharePoint. Users can view and refresh diagrams – in a browser. You can integrate your Visio diagrams into SharePoint, and develop rich mash-ups and applications. What are some other things you can do with Visio integration? You might be surprised.

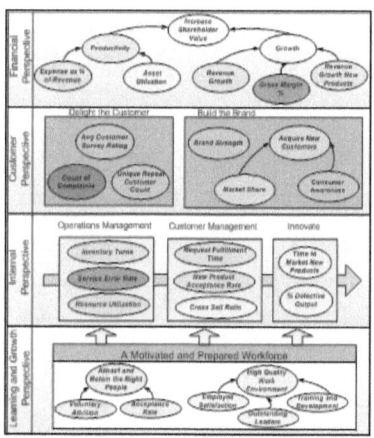

**Visio Data Visualization**

Imagine your trade show floor maps with real-time information about which booths are sold and which are available. Trade show floor maps that show traffic. Feed your ID scanner information into Visio to show which booths are busy during specific times.

These are not typical reports – these are visualizations using Visio. Visio Services lets you publish them to executives, staff, members, volunteers, attendees, vendors, or to anyone you wish.

## Access Services

Deploy your Access databases in SharePoint. No more complicated file shares or FTP sites (ugh). No more sending out copies of your Access database on disks, CDs, or thumb drives.

How many Microsoft Access applications are floating around your org today? Are these applications delicately balanced and located so they can be shared while people are in the office? Publish these applications *directly* in SharePoint. Give users the ability to use a web browser to interface with these applications using Access Services. You already have the applications. You already have the skills to update and manage the applications in Access. Use the skills you already have.

## InfoPath Forms Services

SharePoint alone lets you create simple forms for capturing and validating data. InfoPath lets you create *complex* forms. An example of a complex form is one with repeating sections, like a travel itinerary with multiple legs, or an expense report that can expand with multiple line items.

Complex forms are easy to create in InfoPath. The problem with InfoPath is the end user needs InfoPath to view and fill out the forms – just like a PDF. If you post a PDF form, your users must have a PDF reader installed.

InfoPath Forms Services lets you publish your complex InfoPath forms without requiring anyone to install InfoPath, or an InfoPath Viewer. InfoPath Forms Services gives you the tools to publish these forms to SharePoint. Your users interact with these forms using nothing but a browser.

## PowerPivot for SharePoint

If you haven't yet seen PowerPivot for Excel 2010, it might be worth a look. PowerPivot for Excel gives you the power to create rich and powerful BI tools for analysis – directly from Excel. You can easily load MASSIVE amounts of data from any data source. Slick.

| 2007 | 2008 | 2009 | Grand Total |
|---|---|---|---|
| $ 13,280,564.07 | $ 15,793,026.90 | $ 11,101,750.39 | $ 40,175,341.36 |
| $ 250,420,400.10 | $ 215,517,120.02 | $ 119,570,121.52 | $ 585,507,641.64 |
| $ 98,958,983.98 | $ 64,720,618.78 | $ 66,347,269.56 | $ 230,026,872.32 |
| $ 362,319,447.63 | $ 252,359,036.74 | $ 270,312,661.87 | $ 884,991,146.24 |
| $ 13,326,711.99 | $ 8,689,338.03 | $ 7,104,545.77 | $ 29,120,595.79 |
| $ 391,159,756.57 | $ 356,565,065.86 | $ 365,090,253.85 | $ 1,112,815,076.28 |
| $ 45,023,177.05 | $ 33,027,086.32 | $ 17,575,392.32 | $ 95,625,655.69 |
|  | $ 39,183,456.62 | $ 66,384,514.26 | $ 105,567,970.88 |
| $ 1,174,489,041.39 | $ 985,854,749.27 | $ 923,486,509.54 | $ 3,083,830,300.20 |

**PowerPivot for Excel**

PowerPivot for SharePoint surfaces your PowerPivot for Excel application to an entire team via SharePoint. Share and collaborate on user-generated models in the browser.

## Advanced Business Data Integration

Remember the Business Connectivity Services that comes in every version of SharePoint 2010? Well, SharePoint Server 2010 Enterprise delivers a few more tools to interact with external data.

First, you get a Data Connection Library to centralize the management of all of those connections. Your business users do not have to figure out connection strings to start using the SharePoint tools. Once the connections are in the library, you can use them.

SharePoint also provides Business Data Web Parts to surface that data **without writing a single line of code**. These Web Parts can be used to construct full-fledged membership directories, event listings, product listings, and other information you want to publish from your existing databases. With SharePoint, say goodbye to writing miles of code.

The Business Data Web Parts let you search, filter, and sort data from your external databases without writing code. These Web Parts can display full listings or individual record details. These Web Parts can even show parent-child relationships with data – again **without writing code**.

Finally, SharePoint Server 2010 Enterprise allows Business Data Integration with Office Clients. You can access and really use your existing business application data directly within Office 2010 applications like Word and Excel. You can use it for automatically connecting data for lookups, metadata, contracts, invoices, purchase orders, or nearly *anything* you can imagine – directly from the Office client.

**Even More Search Enhancements**

Search is covered in greater detail later. Just know that SharePoint Server 2010 Enterprise gives you Visual Best Bets, Thumbnails,

Previews, Tunable Search Relevance, Rich Web Indexing, and Deep Search Refinements.

**Business Intelligence**

SharePoint Server 2010 Enterprise is an integral part of the Business Intelligence solution from Microsoft. Business Intelligence Center, PerformancePoint Services, Decomposition Tree, Calculated Key Performance Indicator, and Chart Web Parts all contribute to providing one of the most powerful and user friendly BI tools available anywhere at any price.

These tools are included with your SharePoint Server 2010 Enterprise license. These are not add-ons or extras. They're just in there.

| Sales Scorecard | | | | | | | ▾ |
|---|---|---|---|---|---|---|---|
| | Actual | | Target | | | Trend | |
| ⊟ Internet Sales Amount | | | △ | | | ⇧ | |
| ⊞ Pulleys | $667,015 | $700,760 | △ | -5% | 700759.96 | ⇧ | -5% |
| ⊞ Bikes | $15,483,926 | $34,080,279 | ◈ | -55% | 28318144.6507 | ⇧ | -45% |
| ⊞ Differentials | $322,677 | $339,773 | △ | -5% | 339772.61 | ⇧ | -5% |

**Example Dashboard Scorecard**

Microsoft has changed BI. Traditionally, BI solutions were extremely expensive, costlier to actually implement, and were only used by a handful of executives at an org.

Using SharePoint for your BI puts the power of business intelligence in the hands of all of your users. Provide the right information to the right people at the right time. These are not canned reports. SharePoint provides **real** analysis tools.

| Operations Detail | Q1 CY 2004 | | | Q2 CY 2004 | | |
|---|---|---|---|---|---|---|
| | Actual | Target | Trend | Actual | Target | Trend |
| **Revenues** | | | | | | |
| Revenue | $11,386,315 | $11,386,315 | 0% ⬇ | $14,371,807 | $14,371,807 | 0% ⬆ |
| Channel Revenue | $7,102,685 | $8,051,000 | -12% ⬇ | $8,935,377 | $10,359,000 | -14% ⬆ |
| Internet Revenue | $4,283,630 | $4,283,630 | 0% ⬇ | $5,436,429 | $5,436,429 | 0% ⬆ |
| **Sales** | | | | | | |
| Sales Amount | $11,386,315 | $14,613,989 | -22% ⬇ | $14,371,807 | $12,524,947 | 15% ⬆ |
| Internet Sales Amount | $4,283,630 | $4,283,630 | 0% ⬇ | $5,436,429 | $5,436,429 | 0% ⬆ |
| Sales Qty | 31,517 | 46,426 | -32% ⬇ | 43,669 | 34,669 | 26% ⬆ |
| Avg Sales Amt | $1,872 | $2,461 | -24% ⬇ | $2,087 | $2,059 | 1% ⬆ |
| Reseller Avg Sales Amt | $15,997 | $22,525 | -29% ⬇ | $19,856 | $17,597 | 13% ⬆ |
| **Margins** | | | | | | |
| Gross Profit Margin | 15.77% | 18.0% | -12% ⬇ | 15.39% | 18.0% | -14% ⬆ |
| Reseller Gross Profit Margin | 0.3% | 5.0% | -94% ⬇ | -0.4% | 5.0% | -108% ⬆ |
| Expense to Revenue Ratio | 24.6% | 18.0% | -37% ⬇ | 19.8% | 18.0% | -10% ⬆ |

**Example Dashboard with Key Performance Indicators**

You can use dashboards and the BI tools to analyze membership, commerce, event attendance, event registration, marketing, booth sales, product sales, and any other data that you have. Look at trending, comparative analysis, decomposition of the data, drill down, drill up, and perform real analysis of the data. Turn your raw data into information. Use your information to share knowledge. Educate your executives, staff, members, volunteers, donors, members, and even the public.

## Summary

Microsoft has three different versions of SharePoint that provide incrementally more functionality.

**SharePoint Foundation 2010** is free and can be used internally, externally, and everywhere in between. SharePoint Foundation is perfect for team-based collaboration but is capable of so much more.

**SharePoint Server 2010 Standard** adds enterprise features, web content management, and social networking.

**SharePoint Server 2010 Enterprise** adds BI, Office Services (Access, Visio, Excel, and InfoPath), advanced data integration, and more Search capabilities.

# SharePoint 101: Orientation

There are hundreds of books that detail every technical aspect of SharePoint. There are already books detailing how to install, configure, administer, and write code for SharePoint. We are not attempting to recreate any of those books. SharePoint 101 is a high level overview of capabilities and specific terminologies.

Microsoft "borrowed" a lot of very common words for use in SharePoint: Sites, Lists, Libraries, Workflow, Pages, Items, Columns, and Content Types. These words have very specific meanings within the context of SharePoint. We've capitalized every SharePoint-specific term throughout the book to make learning SharePoint easier.

Let's start at a very high level. What are some of the features that make SharePoint interesting for an org?

## Browser Support

This is big. A business or government agency can dictate what platform their users access their websites with. Orgs do not have control over their users' computers. At the very least, they know what browsers their users have. Orgs do not have this luxury. Orgs have users everywhere on the planet. Members, donors, volunteers, and Joe Public use whatever browser they want. You can't ask them to change anything.

The good news is that you *can* use SharePoint with Safari, Firefox, and Internet Explorer. You can use Windows, Mac, or Linux OS.

You can use a desktop, laptop, or mobile device. You can use SharePoint with an iPad. SharePoint provides a solution that works across platforms and across browsers.

Can users access all content? Yes. Can users participate in content creation? Yes. Can users collaborate? Yes. Can users search for content, view websites, update calendars, add documents, manage tasks, and do what they need to do using the technology? Yes.

Can every user do absolutely everything that is possible in SharePoint from any browser on any platform? No. SharePoint has some advanced capabilities which require specific client applications. For example, SharePoint has very tight Microsoft Office integration. Users who do not have Microsoft Office cannot utilize Office integration; nonetheless, they can still download documents.

If there are users that interact with your org who don't have Microsoft Office, SharePoint has a solution. SharePoint 2010 has "Office Web Applications" which allows users to not only view, but actually work with Office documents such as Word, Excel and PowerPoint – from within their browser. How many other platforms offer this capability? If you count SharePoint, there is exactly one.

## Mobile

SharePoint has built-in mobile support. Previous versions of SharePoint had "some" mobile capabilities as well, but this has been significantly improved.

We think one of the best new features for enabling near real-time updates and collaboration is the integration of texting! SharePoint allows SMS Alerts to be sent. Users can self-subscribe to receive an Alert notification when something changes. Alerts can be email messages or SMS-based messages (text messages).

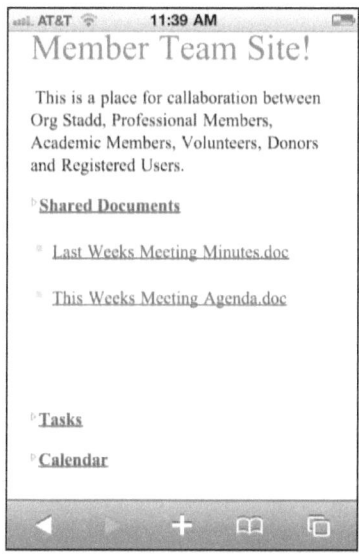

**SharePoint 2010 Team Site on iPhone 4**

SharePoint provides a *very* lightweight interface to your SharePoint content. Use your mobile device for accessing Document Libraries, Lists, Wikis, Blogs, and Web Part Pages. Your mobile users can also access your backend data or Line of Business (LOB) systems. What does that even mean?

It means SharePoint can provide a mobile interface to your member database, your AMS, or your CRM. From a mobile device, you can view member details and member records. Users can have full access to a member directory – from their phone.

SharePoint also provides viewers for Word, Excel and PowerPoint documents. Users can read and search within these Office documents. The ability to search from a mobile device is important. Using a 200-page word document on a phone is cumbersome at best, regardless of the specific smartphone you holster. SharePoint allows users to search for a keyword, and delivers search results yielding deep links directly into the document. Very powerful.

The SharePoint Search experience has been optimized for mobile as well. Finding people, finding content stored in SharePoint, finding information in documents, and finding data in your custom databases (AMS) are supported with mobility views in SharePoint.

# SharePoint 2010 Search on iPhone 4

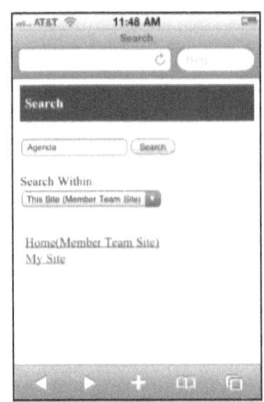
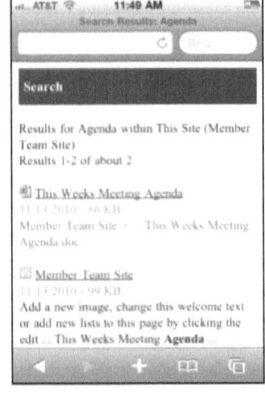
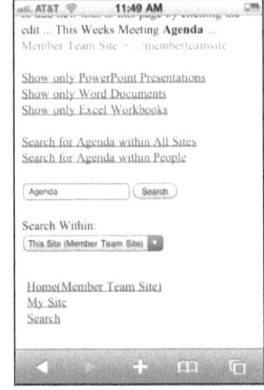

Mobile Search          Search Results          More Search Tools

Finally, SharePoint provides a mobile version of the My Site. Status updates, posts, tags, and more are available in the mobile version of the My Site. Don't worry if you don't know what a My Site is yet, we'll cover it very soon.

## Accessibility

SharePoint has built-in support for accessibility standards (also known as Section 508 compliance or WCAG Level 2 compliance). SharePoint has built-in support for keyboard navigation. Previous versions of SharePoint did not have this, SharePoint 2010 provides this natively.

## Multilingual

Before we dive into multilingual features, let's be very clear about something. SharePoint does not automatically translate your content into a different language. This is asked so frequently and misunderstood by so many people that it is worth repeating.

**SharePoint does not translate your English text into Spanish or any other language.**

SharePoint can manage the process by which you translate the content (either manually or automatically), but SharePoint does not do the translation.

SharePoint is used around the world and is built with support for various languages using two distinct support concepts. The first concept is language Variations.

Variations may be utilized if your org is using SharePoint for a public-facing website and you require various pages within the website to be available in multiple languages. Variations facilitate the management and maintenance of content for different users. Variations can be based on different languages, countries, or regions. Variations can also be used to represent different brands or devices. If your org actually has affiliate orgs which are managed in a similar fashion, you can use SharePoint Variations to represent that content in a different way for different users.

The other concept is based on Language Packs. Language Packs are provided by Microsoft and allow you to use SharePoint in a different language. This means your entire user experience. Site navigation, Site menus, and the SharePoint Ribbon are all available in the selected language. SharePoint search also uses the language information. Users creating Sites have the option to select the default language of the site. SharePoint will automatically detect the browser language preference and react appropriately. Users may also select the desired language.

## Site

One of the fundamental concepts in SharePoint is the Site. A Site is just a collection of "stuff." A Site is a collection of information. A Site can contain Documents, Pages, Lists, Libraries, Calendars, images, media, videos, CAD files – pretty much any kind of content that you can imagine. A Site has unique security properties. A Site can be locked down to a specific team of people, or opened to the entire world by allowing anonymous access. A Site can be stand alone or nested within other Sites (sometimes called Subsites). Subsites can be thought of as sections. Sites can utilize different languages. Subsites can have distinct language settings which are different from their parent Site.

Sites can be manipulated very easily using a web browser. You can change the Theme (which changes the color scheme and fonts). You can change the navigation. You can add and hide links. You can add structures for content. Sites can be manipulated by adding Lists, Libraries, Workflow, Security, Content Types, Page Layouts, Master Pages, and many more components. Finally, after you have manipulated a Site to satisfy your requirements – you can save your Site as a Site Template.

Some Sites are intended to be permanent fixtures which are always available, like your main Intranet page or your public-facing website. Some Sites are intended to be disposable, used only for a short time, such as a Site dedicated to a project or an event. In either case, you have the capability to move or delete Sites with ease.

All SharePoint Sites are based on Site Templates. Even if you want to create an empty Site, it is created from a Site Template cleverly named "Blank Site." There are different Site Templates depending on the version of SharePoint you choose, and the Templates are available in all flavors: Team Site, Blog, Document Center, Meeting Workspace, Search Center, Enterprise Wiki, Publishing Portal, and more. Site Templates are a powerful tool in SharePoint.

As explained earlier, Sites can be manipulated. You can always manipulate various aspects of the Site should your org's requirements change.

The following list details configurable Site options:

➤ **Language**. Text that appears on the Site is displayed in the Site Template's language.

➢ **Security**. Define unique user groups and permissions for each Site.

➢ **Navigation**. Configure unique navigation links in each part of your SharePoint hierarchy. Site navigation can reflect relationships among the Sites in a Site Collection.

➢ **Web Pages**. Customize pages associated with various Sites.

➢ **Layouts**. Provide unique layouts or master pages in a Site.

➢ **Themes**. Modify colors and fonts on a Site.

➢ **Regional settings**. Modify the regional settings, such as locale, time zone, sort order, time format, and calendar type.

➢ **Search**. Customize search settings. For example, specify that a particular Site never appears in search results.

➢ **Content Types**. Customize each Site's Content Types and Site Columns (metadata).

➢ **Workflows**. Provide unique workflows for each Site.

## Pages

A Page is really just HTML content and (optionally) some Web Parts. At its core, a SharePoint Site is exposed through a Page. A

Page is just like any web page that you have ever seen – the common building block that is found around the World Wide Web.

A SharePoint Page is what you see in the web browser, regardless if you are using a Windows, Mac, or smartphone browser. There are a couple of types of Pages in SharePoint, and each of these types has unique benefits. There are Wiki Pages, Publishing Pages, and cleverly named Web Part Pages. Rather than digging into the details of different types of Pages here, just know that the Page is one of the ways SharePoint surfaces content to users.

## Lists

Now let's look at Lists. Many people understand what a database table is. If not, you've probably used a spreadsheet. You can really think of a List as being similar. A List is just as the name implies – it is a list of data. A List is made up of columns and rows. A List can be extremely simple. The simplest List in SharePoint displays just a single column called "Title."

Let's say that you need an area to store the names of all of the states where your org has Chapters. You can create a List! You would browse to the List, and click Create. You would see a new form that has a single text box. You could type in "Virginia" and click the button to submit. Voila! You have now added an Item to your List.

Of course, Lists can be more sophisticated than a single text field. Just like an Excel spreadsheet, you can add many fields to your List that allow you to store the exact type of information that you need.

SharePoint provides a series of List Templates to help get you started. For example, SharePoint has a List Template for Announcements. An Announcement List has three fields: Title, Description, and Expiration Date. The Announcement List is for managing announcements for users of a particular SharePoint Site. You can use a Web Part to publish these announcements on the main Page of the SharePoint Site. Brilliant!

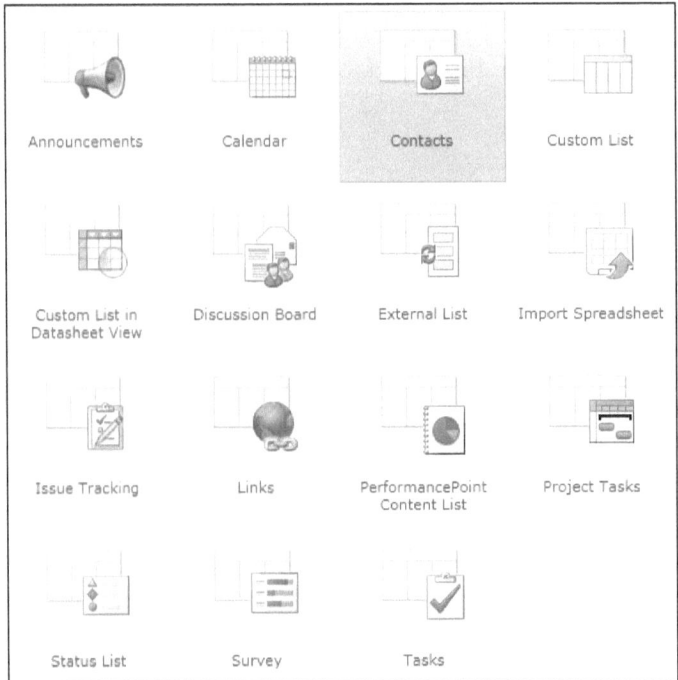

**SharePoint 2010 Lists**

SharePoint also provides Lists for Contacts, Calendars, Links, Tasks, Surveys, Discussion Boards, and more. If you need to add or remove fields associated with any of the Lists, you can do this through the web browser.

## Library

A Library is a List that specializes in managing documents. The documents can be Office Documents (Word, Excel, PowerPoint, etc.), PDFs, Images, or nearly any type of file you can think of. Video files, audio files, podcasts, CAD files, text files, and Zip files can all be stored in Libraries.

**Document Library**

## Item

An Item equates to a row in a traditional spreadsheet or database table. An Item represents a single entry into a List (or Library).

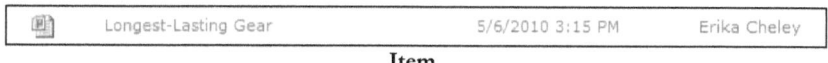

**Item**

## Lists and Libraries

You can organize List Items into Folders within a List or Document Library. You can then use a View to show the Folders or flatten the Items out into a single, large display. Lists, by default, are included in Search results. You can optionally hide a List form the search entirely.

# Column

As we mentioned earlier, Lists can be comprised of much more than just a single text field. SharePoint allows you to create new fields in a SharePoint List or Library by adding Columns. The capacity for you to add Columns is almost limitless.

Let's say you wanted to capture a list of people who stop by your booth at a tradeshow. First, you create a new List called "Booth Attendees." You then create a new Column for full name, a Column for email address, a Column for mailing address, and maybe a Column for comments that would allow you to type a few notes about the person who stopped by. That's it! Now you have a database that will store all of your contacts from the tradeshow. As a side note, you could have just created a new List using the Contacts List Template and saved even more time!

When you create a List in SharePoint, you get a lot more. SharePoint also creates your interfaces. You get a web form for entering Items into your List, and for editing existing Items. You get Pages that let you view Items one at a time. You get a Page that lets you see, edit, and delete Items in a grid, called a Datasheet View.

```
Column name:
┌─────────────────────────────────────────┐
│Committee                                 │
└─────────────────────────────────────────┘

The type of information in this column is:
  ⦿ Single line of text
  ○ Multiple lines of text
  ○ Choice (menu to choose from)
  ○ Number (1, 1.0, 100)
  ○ Currency ($, ¥, €)
  ○ Date and Time
  ○ Lookup (information already on this site)
  ○ Yes/No (check box)
  ○ Person or Group
  ○ Hyperlink or Picture
  ○ Calculated (calculation based on other columns)
  ○ External Data
  ○ Managed Metadata
```

**Column Types**

You get tools to view, filter, and sort items. SharePoint provides filtering and sorting on Columns in the List. If you wanted to sort by attendee name, you click the "name" column header and sort alphabetically or reverse-alphabetical. If "state" were one of the Columns, filter with two clicks to display items where "state" is equal to Texas.

Impressed, aren't you? Sounds like Microsoft took what we've been doing for years in Excel and added it to SharePoint. For good reason, Excel is a great tool with powerful capabilities. SharePoint Lists and Libraries utilize these powerful capabilities; but as you will see, the possibilities extend beyond that of a flat spreadsheet.

## Item Versioning

Within each Item in a List or Library, SharePoint has the ability to track changes. Who changed it? Which field was changed? When was it changed? You can view previous versions of List Items, and even restore previous Versions.

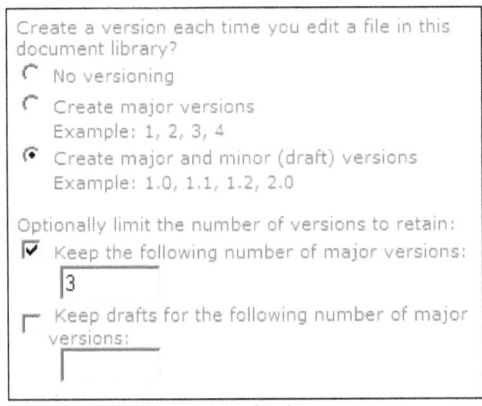

Create a version each time you edit a file in this document library?
- ○ No versioning
- ○ Create major versions
  Example: 1, 2, 3, 4
- ● Create major and minor (draft) versions
  Example: 1.0, 1.1, 1.2, 2.0

Optionally limit the number of versions to retain:
- ☑ Keep the following number of major versions:
  3
- ☐ Keep drafts for the following number of major versions:

**Version Options**

What does this mean? It means when using a Document Library, SharePoint can keep a Version of each file change. If Bill creates a Document and then Sally changes the Document, SharePoint allows you to see and compare both Versions of the document – both the current, and all previous Versions. This works for Document Libraries and Lists. You can also limit the amount of Versions to retain.

## List Views

List Views are another feature of SharePoint Lists and Libraries. Views are different ways of displaying the data contained within your List or Library. Database administrators will be very familiar with this concept because it's quite similar to a view of a database table.

A View shows only specific columns you wish to see. Lists may have multiple Views. A View can be a Personal View or a Public View. Personal Views are for you and you alone. Public Views are shared for others to see as well. Views support Filters, Grouping, Column Totals, Folders, Styling, Inline Editing, Paging, and Mobile Views.

## Export to Excel

With a single click of the mouse, you can Export your List data to Excel. Business users appreciate this because they already live in Excel. Your users can slice, dice, pivot, and chart the data from SharePoint to their heart's content using Excel.

## Open with Access

You can also export your List data to Access. It gets even better. You can link data in real time with Microsoft Access.

What does that mean, and why should you care?

It means you can use Access Reports to provide easy to generate, branded, and printable reports on virtually any data stored in SharePoint. With Business Connectivity Services, the data can even be stored elsewhere and surfaced in SharePoint. Furthermore, Access will actually allow users to update information linked in SharePoint.

You can also use Access to link to multiple SharePoint Lists simultaneously. You can actually use Access to construct a client front-end to a complex application which is storing data in SharePoint Lists. So, what is the real power of this tight integration? You can do all of this without writing a single line of code.

## Web Part

Let's go straight to Microsoft to quote their definition: A Web Part is a modular unit of information that forms a basic building block of most pages on a site.

Wow, that is clear! It is tough to articulate the supreme power of a Web Part in just one sentence so let's expand on that a bit.

A Web Part is a widget. A Web Part is a small rectangle (usually) that displays content. A Web Part could show content from somewhere else on your Site. A Web Part could show content from other websites. A Web Part could aggregate content from any of your SharePoint Sites.

SharePoint ships with a lot of Web Parts. You can configure your own Web Parts. There are Web Parts which may be downloaded for free. There are lots of companies that specialize in building and selling custom Web Parts.

Web Parts allow for advanced configuration and customization – directly from the web browser. There is a gallery of Web Parts in every SharePoint environment. By managing the Web Parts in the Web Part Gallery, you determine which Web Parts are allowed to be used within your SharePoint environment. You may wish to disallow particular Web Parts (like external RSS feeds), or install new Web Parts (like any of those available from the open source community or third-party vendors).

**Insert a Web Part**

Some Web Parts allow interaction with Lists and Libraries. There are Web Parts that provide content aggregation. There are Web Parts for personalization, Dashboards, business data (external databases), Filters, Search, Picture Libraries, RSS feeds, and many more Web Parts. The default Search and Search Results experience in SharePoint is configured using Search Web Parts.

You can add Web Parts to Pages in SharePoint very easily. By using the Ribbon Toolbar interface in SharePoint, you can Edit a Page and then insert a Web Part. Yes. It is that easy.

## List and Library Web Parts

You remember Web Parts, right? Those widgets you can put on a Page, drag and drop, connect to other Web Parts, personalize the Views, etc. Sure you do. We just talked about them.

Well, guess what? Every List and Library that you create in SharePoint automatically gets Web Parts that you can use throughout your SharePoint Site. You can create a View of any List, and then show it on a Page using a Web Part.

You can have a single Page that shows multiple Web Parts. These Web Parts could each point to different Views of the same SharePoint List. You could have different Web Parts that point to different SharePoint Lists and Libraries.

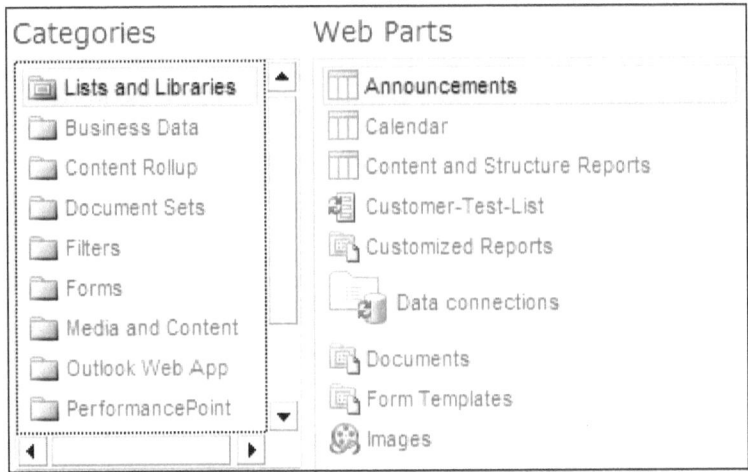

**Web Part Categories**

Let's say you are using a SharePoint Site based on the Site Template called Team Site. This Team Site is being used by your IT team on the Intranet. This Site has a List for announcements, another List for project tasks, a List for vendor contacts, and a Document Library for standard operating procedures. You can aggregate all of this information into a single Page on the Team Site. You can have Web Parts that show current announcements, unfinished tasks, recently edited documents, and recent vendors who have been contacted. SharePoint makes it easy to aggregate all of this content into a single Page using Web Parts.

This is just one example. These List and Library Web Parts can be used in hundreds of combinations to build dynamic Views of active work. Project work, knowledge bases, Calendar Views, project management work schedules, program management Sites, education Sites, and many other examples are possible. The best part – it's all configurable from the browser. You do not need a developer (or an IT Pro) to make this happen.

## Alerts

Alerts are notifications. Alerts are either email notifications or SMS (text-messaging) notifications. Users can self-subscribe to receive an Alert notification when anything in a List or Library has changed. If another user adds, updates, or deletes any Item in the List, the subscribed user will receive a notification (Alert) with a link directly to the changed Item. In fact, users can subscribe to a single Item in the list! If anyone changes that single item, an alert will be sent to the subscribed users.

Imagine your team working together on defining new standards or fundraising material in a Document Library. Rather than having to email each other or constantly checking the Site for updated documents, SharePoint will automatically send an Alert when the content has been updated. Immediate notifications allow users to stay passively connected at all times.

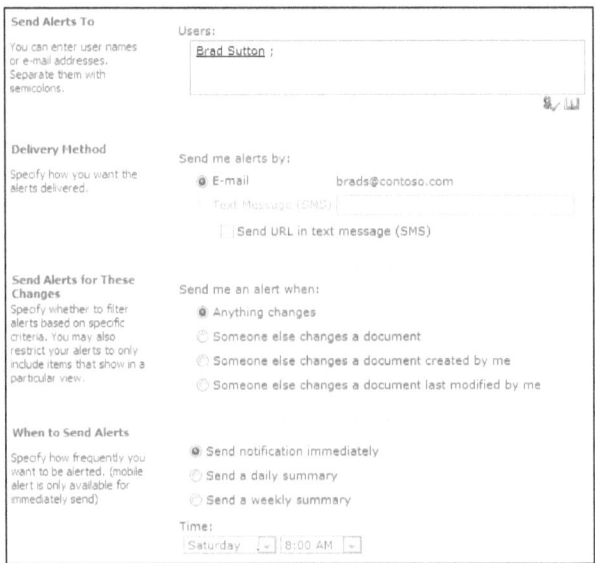

**Sign Up for an Alert**

Users also have the ability to configure Alerts with Search, and SharePoint will notify the subscribing user when new content is indexed matching the keyword(s) they were searching for.

## RSS Feeds

Lists and Libraries can provide an RSS feed of your data based on a View. You can have a List of news articles, announcements, prices, availability, or any other information you wish to syndicate using RSS. Creating the List and having the RSS feed immediately available can be accomplished with a few mouse clicks in the browser. RSS feeds can be syndicated from other content as well, such as Search Results or even using the Content Query Web Part – that silver bullet Web Part that can aggregate content from across multiple SharePoint Sites.

You can also display RSS feeds from other locations without writing code with a Web Part.

```
┌─────────────────────────────────────┐
│  ⊟  RSS Properties                   │
│                                       │
│  RSS Feed URL                         │
│  ─────────────────────────────────   │
│  ..................................   │
│  Feed refresh time (in minutes)       │
│                                 120   │
│  ..................................   │
│  Feed Limit                           │
│                                   5   │
│  ..................................   │
│  ☐  Show feed title and description   │
└─────────────────────────────────────┘
```

**Add an RSS Web Part**

The RSS Viewer Web Part lets you specify an RSS feed URL and the number of items you wish to display. Make your SharePoint Site a true portal containing relevant content – whether you are actually creating the content or not.

## SharePoint Workspace

Workspace is the new Groove. Prior to SharePoint 2010, SharePoint Workspace was called Groove. SharePoint Workspace allows you to take your SharePoint data offline, modify offline data as needed, and then automatically synchronize this data with your org's SharePoint environment once you're back online.

If you sync a List (or Library or an entire Site) to SharePoint Workspace, you can take a copy of your content on the road with you – without being connected to SharePoint. When you are back online, SharePoint Workspace will synchronize your changes automatically with the changes others have made. We've seen SharePoint Workspace save the day for orgs with field operatives without constant internet connectivity. Executives and senior staff who travel appreciate how SharePoint Workspace keeps important information at their fingertips.

## Security

Security has a dedicated chapter, but it's important to point out a List can have its own security. Even more granular, an Item within a List can have unique security as well. By default, a List inherits permissions from the Site which contains it. A List Item inherits permissions from List which contains it. You can change all of that. You can define distinct permissions for a List. You can define which users can read, update, create, and delete List Items.

## Templates

Let's say you've been building out a new SharePoint Site for a committee. You've spent some time perfecting your List. You've added some Columns. You've created six different Views to help the team. You've populated the list with some initial data. You've got it set exactly how you need it. Wouldn't it be great if you could copy this List for use elsewhere? You can. Simply copy the List to use again. You can even save your List as a Template.

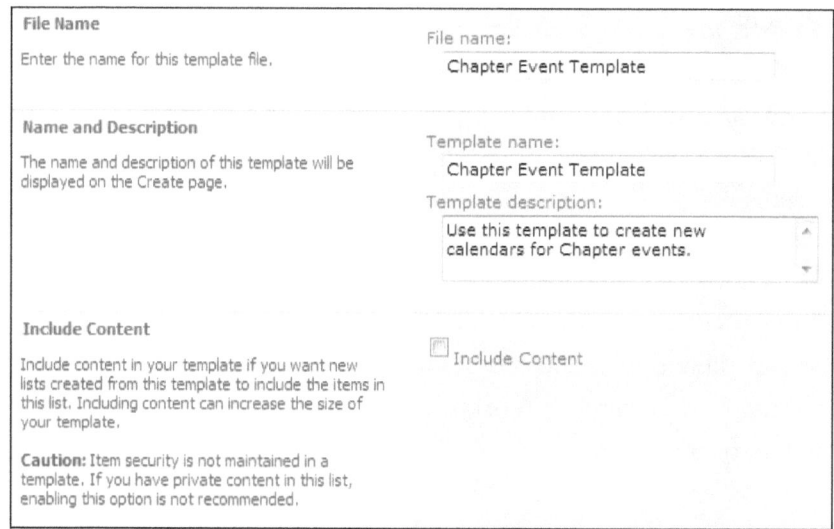

| File Name | |
| --- | --- |
| Enter the name for this template file. | File name:<br>Chapter Event Template |
| **Name and Description** | |
| The name and description of this template will be displayed on the Create page. | Template name:<br>Chapter Event Template<br>Template description:<br>Use this template to create new calendars for Chapter events. |
| **Include Content** | |
| Include content in your template if you want new lists created from this template to include the items in this list. Including content can increase the size of your template.<br><br>**Caution:** Item security is not maintained in a template. If you have private content in this list, enabling this option is not recommended. | ☐ Include Content |

**Save List as a Template**

SharePoint makes extensive use of Templates. While Site Templates were described previously, List Templates are another great feature of SharePoint. It's easy to build a List, save it as a Template, and then create a new List based on your List Template. *Note:* There are multiple ways to capture attendee information within SharePoint, and this is just one example.

## Workflow

We work with orgs which utilize SharePoint solely for the powerful Workflow capabilities. They do not use SharePoint for public-facing websites as they are already using something else like Wordpress, Ektron, or Sitecore. *Oh, the horror! Supporting so many technologies is a waste of precious resources!* Still, the fact that these orgs would use SharePoint solely for Workflow is a testament to the truly impressive nature of SharePoint's Workflow functionality.

Workflow is a series of Actions defined by conditional statements. A Workflow can be used to approve content publishing, manage language translation, and update data. A Workflow can also be used for reviewing and approving documents, or for archiving purposes.

Workflows can send email notifications based on conditional logic. Workflows can assign tasks. Workflows may be triggered by events such as new documents being created, documents being uploaded, modified, or deleted. Workflows can be based on time, human action, or information.

So how does this help your org? Workflows can be used to manage certification processing, abstract submission processes, grant management, project management tasks, membership applications, and many more automated activities.

There are three levels of Workflow creation within SharePoint. You can actually create simple Workflows directly in the browser. If you need more flexibility, you can create more complex Workflows in SharePoint Designer. If you need the ultimate in-workflow sophistication, you can get a developer to create SharePoint Workflows in Visual Studio. Save the Visual Studio option as an absolute last resort.

Much of what you will need to do is easily accomplished without writing code. Even if you can't figure out how to configure (as opposed to customizing), there are many third-party add-ins for creating SharePoint Workflows. Evaluate using third-party tools before you walk down the path of custom code development and maintenance – even if you have developers on your staff.

You can configure a large majority of the Workflows your org will need using SharePoint Designer. We are HUGE fans of using SharePoint Designer. You can develop, deploy, and mange entire applications using SharePoint Designer – all without writing a single line of code.

## Business Connectivity Services

Business Connectivity Services (BCS) is an incredible technology. Even if you didn't use SharePoint for anything else, SharePoint is worth its weight in gold because of BCS.

BCS allows you to interact with external data. BCS provides the user interface, the security model, and the connectivity interfaces for using back end data.

**Add New Data Source**

You can use BCS to easily connect to databases, Web and Windows Communication Foundation (WCF) services, Microsoft .NET connectivity assemblies, and custom data sources.

What do we mean by "easily?" We mean SharePoint Designer provides a wizard. First you connect to an external database, then you select a table (or database view or procedure), and then select the properties. Voila! SharePoint then provides you with CRUDQ operations using the familiar SharePoint interface. CRUDQ is Create, Read, Update, Delete, and Query.

BCS allows you to build mashups and composites. BCS allows you to surface your member data or financial data, yet keep it restricted only to the users who should have access –without writing any code.

BCS allows you to use Workflows, Search, use mobile devices, leverage Content Types, Permissions, and all the other cool things SharePoint does – but it uses data located outside of SharePoint.

As you can imagine, BCS is a technology big enough for a book on its own. There are plenty of books, blogs, samples, and even third-party tools for working with BCS which you can explore.

## Summary

Even with a high level overview of the fundamental concepts of SharePoint, you should start to see the potential of using SharePoint for your org. SharePoint is commonly used by orgs for intranets, extranets, social communities, and public-facing websites. SharePoint is a powerful business platform with many implications. Understanding the core SharePoint capabilities is the first step when determining how to best leverage SharePoint within your org.

# Plan for SharePoint Success

You may have picked up on this already; we are *huge* fans of SharePoint. We like the technology, but we love the solutions. It's very exciting to see the benefits SharePoint provides to organizations just like yours.

Amidst this excitement, it's important to resist the urge to *implement SharePoint*. You should not just *implement SharePoint*. Rather, you should leverage SharePoint as a platform to *implement a specific solution for your org*.

Nothing in this world is one-size-fits-all anymore. Did you know Starbucks has more than 19,000 ways to serve a cup of coffee? If you've ever stood in a line at Starbucks, you've heard patrons order from this staggering combination of beans, syrup, and milk. They order things that are clearly not on the menu, and they use a language of their own.

SharePoint is even more flexible. It has a language of its own. SharePoint has exponentially more configuration possibilities and puts power in the hands of every authorized user. You do not have to be a trained barista to use SharePoint; you just need a username.

What makes this example particularly relevant? Starbucks uses SharePoint, too.

SharePoint is vastly different than any typical software. For example, to implement antivirus software, you just install it and it works. You may have to schedule some virus definition updates or schedule it to scan your computer, but it's easy.

SharePoint is highly configurable and can be leveraged in many different ways. Sure, you *can* just install SharePoint and have a website. Many orgs do. An IT Pro installs SharePoint and announces, "We now have SharePoint."

This approach may gain some efficiency, but your org will not reap the full benefits of SharePoint. Farmers don't walk into the woods, throw out a few handfuls of corn and soy, and expect to have a fruitful garden. SharePoint needs careful consideration, thoughtful planning, and organized execution.

Before making an investment of time and resources, before you install the software, you should understand how that investment will support your objectives. Even before you define your objectives, you need to understand your org's strategy.

Your strategy is likely very visible in your org. It may be in the charter, on the wall in the reception area, on your public-facing website, and in the print material you distribute. Your strategy may be synonymous with your mission statement. Your strategy is probably a general collection of ideas explaining the vision of your org. It probably explains how to carry out the mission, and how to generate revenue. It could be about volunteer engagement and membership benefits.

The strategy for your org may be related to growing membership, distributing information, or going after polluters. Regardless, *everything* that you do should support the strategy of your org.

Use your strategy as a guiding principle for defining specific business objectives. Then use your strategy-driven business objectives to define how, when, and where you deploy SharePoint.

Your business objectives do not need to be complex. Business objectives can start very simple, but they do need to support your strategy.

Here are some examples of high level business objectives which are very common with orgs.

We need a better way to:

> ➤ Find information
> ➤ Track and develop new ideas within the organization
> ➤ Provide basic information to new volunteers ‹
> ➤ Manage speaker information
> ➤ Manage abstracts for potential speakers at a conference
> ➤ Track internal projects
> ➤ Manage tasks within departments
> ➤ Track who is working on what
> ➤ Determine conference room availability
> ➤ Provide information to the BOD consistently and easily
> ➤ Update our website without knowing HTML
> ➤ Allow members to give us feedback
> ➤ Allow people to report issues
> ➤ Determine the latest version of a document
> ➤ Determine who contributed to a document

Can SharePoint provide the means for meeting these objectives? It definitely can. These are just some quick examples. Depending on your org's strategy, *your* objectives may differ.

## Business Objectives: Capture, Clarify, Confirm

A traditional software development life cycle (SDLC) may approach requirements with four distinct phases: Gathering, Analyzing, Organizing, and Validating. Depending on the complexity of the initiative, you may even need to determine and quantify other factors such as feasibility, necessity, priority, unambiguousness, verifiable, correctness, completeness, consistency, modifiable, traceable, etc. You get the idea.

For many large projects, a rigid, requirements gathering methodology is critical for success. However, you may not need to follow a traditional SDLC if you are implementing a solution using SharePoint. SharePoint provides such an enormous breadth of capabilities that it may not make sense to start with a blank white board. It may be wiser to frame the business objectives within the context of SharePoint.

What then is the appropriate level of documentation for your business objectives? There is no clear definition or single answer for all orgs. The level of documentation required varies from org to org and from solution to solution. The objectives simply need to be clearly communicated. Everyone on the team needs to be able to understand the objective. Do not spend unnecessary time developing granular requirements which are never going to be used.

As you can see from the above list, it can be easy to capture initial business objectives. Usually, an objective rolls off the tongue using the collective "we" and represents a pain point which needs a solution. It is imperative to make the time to actually clarify and confirm your objectives.

Many people skip the critical step of clarifying objectives. They simply do not make the time to clarify. Unfortunately, a large percentage of failed projects (SharePoint or other) can be traced back to the lack of clear objectives.

Everyone believes they communicate well. Communication involves both "sending" and "receiving." Just because an executive states an objective does not mean it's clearly understood.

Let's look at an example business objective statement: The Executive Director states that the org needs a way for people to report issues.

This objective can be achieved by publishing the cell phone numbers of the org's Support personnel. People can report issues by calling the cell phones of the IT Staff. But which people? All people? Members? Staff? How are the issues classified? Are they phone issues? Website issues? HR issues? Environmental issues? Is it the member's responsibility to classify the issue and assign it to the appropriate resource? Should the member have the ability to view the status of the reported issue? What process is in place to ensure timely response and resolution of issues?

That's likely not what the executive meant at all. The actual desire was to have a web-based form for members to fill out and submit.

So what is the appropriate level of business objective definition for this effort? Do you need to provide 155 bullets to articulate the following type of information?

### Traditional Requirement Definition: The System Shall?

> Requirement 122. User Issue Creation Form. The system shall provide a form that allows creation of a new issue ticket by providing the following fields:

a. Issue Title
- i. Text Field
- ii. 255 characters
- iii. Required.

b. Issue Description
- i. Text
- ii. 1400 characters
- iii. Optional.

c. Issue Type
- i. Drop Down Choice
  1. Choice – Phone Issue
  2. Choice – Laptop Issue
  3. Choice – Hardware Issue
  4. Choice – Software Issue
  5. Choice – Other

Most of the time, you do not need to do this type of requirement definition. In fact, this is counterproductive. It is faster to create this form in SharePoint than it is to fully document all of the fields, options, and ideas. This form can be created within the browser. Once the form has been reviewed, it's easy to modify the form in SharePoint to make it exactly what it needs to be.

The business objectives need to be defined at a level which describes the objective well enough that it can be clarified and understood. Clarification can be simple.

Does the business objective support the strategy of the org? Can the implementation team restate the objectives and still meet the expectations? Can a pilot or prototype be quickly implemented and tested?

After the objective is clarified, it is still important to confirm the objective. Ensure a solution is actually needed. We've seen plenty of great solutions in search of a problem to solve.

What else can you do to help ensure successful implementations?

## Be clear about what SharePoint will do

Can SharePoint be used to construct your accounting system? Absolutely. You can configure the Lists and Libraries in SharePoint to look and behave exactly like an accounting system. You can use custom code to enforce referential integrity, provide extremely robust workflows, enable batch processing, and everything else necessary to run a financial package. Does that mean you should use SharePoint as your accounting package? Probably not.

Just because something is possible does not mean you should do it. The time and effort required to configure SharePoint to make it an accounting system simply cannot be justified when there are so many great off-the-shelf accounting products.

It is equally important to define the boundaries of SharePoint as it is to define the objective. Be clear about what SharePoint will do. And be clear about what SharePoint will *not* do.

SharePoint should not be your financial accounting system. It should not be your network monitoring solution or your email solution. There is no single piece of technology that is all things to all people. Sorry, Steve. Not even the iPad.

## Resist customizing SharePoint

SharePoint is nearly limitless in its capability. Even with a vanilla SharePoint installation, you have a website available that supports collaboration, presentation, searching, and more. SharePoint allows your team to create, aggregate, prioritize, recommend, and deliver content to staff, members, volunteers, or the entire world.

With a little configuration, you can have sophisticated Content Types, Workflow, Alerts, Lists, Libraries, Site Templates, AMS integration, and more. With third-party add-ons, you can have complex Workflows, project management, and completely finished applications, all without ever writing code.

If you do introduce an educated developer, the world is your oyster. SharePoint is capable of being molded into any type of application that you can imagine. The foundation and framework within SharePoint is robust, reliable, and extremely scalable.

SharePoint supports customization. There is a documented API and Web Services interface for developers to use. There are thousands of blog posts related to SharePoint programming. There is sample code available for nearly any type of customization you want to do. So why resist customization?

The majority of your business objectives can be met without customizing SharePoint. You will absolutely need to *configure* SharePoint, but you will likely not need customization.

**You don't need to customize.**

If you are implementing a SharePoint initiative with the idea that you will begin with customization, your org will never realize the full benefits of SharePoint. You will likely build an exact solution that meets the exact needs of the solution defined at that single moment in time. You lose flexibility. You lose control. You become dependent upon a developer to change anything. In essence, you lose SharePoint.

# Choose configuration.

SharePoint configuration exists at three levels: browser configuration, SharePoint Designer configuration, and third-party configuration.

Browser configuration includes all aspects configurable through the native web interface. You can create Sites, Lists, Libraries, Columns, Site Columns, Content Types and Information Management Policies. You can configure User Profiles, Search, Search Results Pages, Search Scopes, Web Parts, Web Part Pages and Publishing Pages. You can create Document Templates, List Templates, Library Templates and Site Templates. That's a lot of stuff. You can build complete applications from within the browser.

SharePoint Designer configuration adds the power to build complex Workflows, configure External Content Types, build Database Connections, and construct Page Layouts and Master Pages. SharePoint Designer lets you easily style SharePoint with new colors, updated navigation elements, and completely new user interface elements.

Utilize third-party configuration and avoid reinventing the wheel. If you need a chat tool, grants management application, listserv, learning management system, SEO plugins, podcasting solution, or any other applications – there may be an existing third-party turnkey solution that meets your needs. It is at the very least worth evaluating a third-party tool before you begin writing code.

## Resist writing custom code.

Resist having a developer write custom code. Use SharePoint for three months without deploying custom code. Learn SharePoint. You really need to *learn* SharePoint. Your IT team needs to *learn* SharePoint. Your developer (if you have one) needs to *experience* SharePoint in order to *really understand* SharePoint.

If you ask your developers to write code in SharePoint before they understand SharePoint, they will. Writing code can be simple. Developers can find sample source code, modify it, and make it work in SharePoint.

We have actually seen a great developer spend weeks (yes, weeks) writing a solution for SharePoint that was perfect! The code was elegant. It achieved the business objectives flawlessly. Guess what? Code was written to do something that SharePoint already did! This developer did not know what SharePoint was capable of and spent weeks developing a solution that SharePoint did natively. **Learn SharePoint.**

SharePoint does not do everything. It does a lot of things but not everything. You may eventually have to write code and deploy custom solutions. *Resist* writing custom code. Leverage the platform fully before you write any custom code. Configure before you customize.

## Executive Sponsorship

SharePoint is a business productivity platform. In order for SharePoint to be widely successful and make an effective change in your organization, you need to plan, execute, and evaluate. Then plan, execute, evaluate. Again. Plan, execute, evaluate. Then do it again.

SharePoint lends itself to an iterative implementation approach. Your org will need governance planning, implementation planning, training, as well as roll out and long-term support. In order to be effective, you need executive buy in. Executive sponsorship ensures the project is given necessary support.

The executive sponsor needs to be an advocate for the organization both inside and out. The executive sponsor should be educated on

SharePoint – what it is, what benefits it will provide, and why your org is using it.

We cannot stress this enough: your executive sponsor needs to be an advocate. No offense to any of the technical people reading this book (we both come from technical backgrounds), but no one wants to hear techie-talk about the benefits of the latest platform being installed. No one cares. It will usually be shrugged off or not taken seriously. People will listen to an executive sponsor. People will want to be involved. People will care.

Many people resist change. People stick with what they know. People like to do what they've always done. Why? That's easy to answer. It's the way they've always done it!

If you want to increase both the efficiency and efficacy of your organization on a massive level, it will take some planning, governance, training, adoption, and discipline. It is definitely worth it. However, it will take commitment. And this level of commitment needs an executive sponsor.

## Findability

Findability is a term used to describe how easy or difficult it is to locate information quickly. Factors which influence findability include the structure and navigation of the Site, Site Search and respective Search Results display, taxonomy content classification, and overall site design (look and feel).

Findability is very, very important. When people are looking for something, they expect to find it immediately. If they cannot find what they are looking for quickly, they get discouraged.

The good news is you have full control over findability. You can make it easy for people to find what they are looking for when you understand what is involved.

Findability can be divided into two main sections: Information Architecture (IA) and Search. IA can be further divided into two sections: Site Structure and Taxonomy.

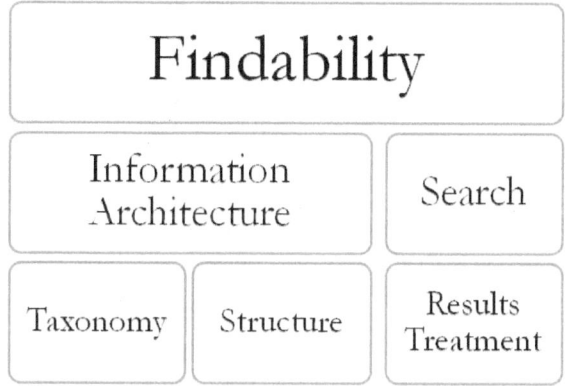

## Information Architecture

Information Architecture (IA) is the structure (where things live) and the taxonomy (metadata) of your content. It is not possible to overstate the importance of your IA. Many failed SharePoint solutions can be tracked back to a poorly implemented or complete lack of Information Architecture. IA includes two main components: Site Structure and Taxonomy.

## Site Structure

Site structure is an important part of your IA. SharePoint IA defines where things live and determines the organization of all Sites contained within Site Collections. To determine the best structure, understand the content that your Site will contain and what will be its relevance to your audiences.

Unearthing the proper Site structure for your org should involve people from various perspectives, and will hopefully involve some healthy debates. Everyone at your org will honestly believe their "stuff" should be on the homepage of the Site because it is of the greatest importance.

During the process of determining where to logically put content, keep in mind that the physical location of a piece of content is not the only way to navigate to it. In SharePoint, it is easy to surface information from across the board and display rollups of similar content based on how it's been tagged or on other similar features. An article may physically reside in a Document Library buried three levels deep in the Site hierarchy, yet an automated List of the five most recent articles can be placed anywhere on the Site – including the home page.

You will likely come across content which is difficult to determine exactly where it should reside. It could even logically be placed in multiple locations.

To determine where the content should physically reside, ask the following questions: Who owns this piece of content? Who is responsible to keep it current? If the answer is "Tom from Communications" then it should physically reside in a location where "Tom from Communications" has ownership permissions.

If the answer is not that simple and many different people are actively involved in keeping this particular content current, ask the following question: Who gets fired if this piece of content is lost? Who is accountable for this content? This is who owns it. Put the content in a place where this person can manage it.

## Taxonomy

Taxonomy refers to the classification of content. It's metadata. In other words, it's data about data. Metadata plays a large role in your IA because it does two very important things.

First, metadata enables you to associate content with other similar pieces of content. Example: Seeing "Related Articles" beside an article on various websites. Metadata facilitates this behavior when related articles have been tagged in a similar fashion as the article being read.

Metadata also enables you to associate content with users. This is also called targeting or personalization. Example: Seeing "Articles You May Be Interested In" or "Upcoming Events You May Be Interested In" which are targeted to specific user profile properties such as interests or events attended.

Taxonomy plays other important roles. Taxonomy influences search results and provides the classification mechanism used for content rollups. If taxonomy tags are to be used for surfacing the five most recent articles related to a given topic, then the articles should be tagged with that topic. This means you need to understand what tags you are going make available to your users. Taxonomy is the very underpinning of a dynamic and smart SharePoint solution.

The first step in the taxonomy process is to identify tags and their logical groupings. There are many innovative ways of determining this information. Whether formal or not, your org likely already has some taxonomy elements determined: issues, topics, certifications, classes, etc. Some of your taxonomy structure may be surfaced during your content assessment due to natural logical groupings.

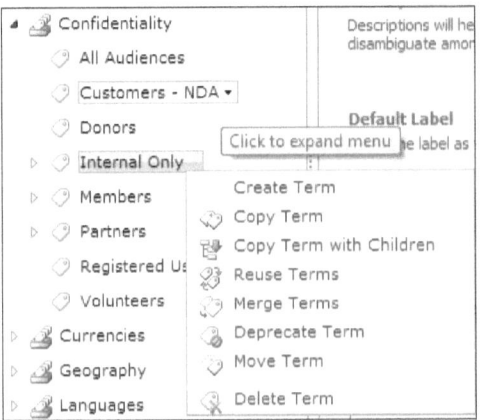

**Manage Taxonomy**

Your taxonomy will likely evolve over time. It is still important to get it as accurate as possible during the early stages of implementation, because the process of re-classifying content is largely manual – without the use of third-party utilities.

Identifying your taxonomy is the hard part, implementing your taxonomy in SharePoint is straight forward.

## Content Organizer

The SharePoint 2010 Content Organizer provides a "drop off library" for users to upload and tag files. Files uploaded into to the drop off library are automatically moved to an appropriate Document Library in the IA hierarchy based on how the file was tagged (classified) at the time of upload.

The Content Organizer Feature simply follows the rules you configure. For example, you may create a rule which says files tagged as "Donor Education" should be moved into a Document Library called "Donor Education Files."

Your SharePoint taxonomy should be carefully crafted in order to take full advantage of its capabilities.

# Migration

You will migrate something into SharePoint. It's inevitable. Here are some examples of migration types:

➢ Previous version of SharePoint to later version (upgrade)

➢ Files and folders from your shared drive into Document Libraries

➢ Web site content

➢ Custom applications

➢ Exchange public folders

➢ Lotus Notes data and/or applications

➢ Other products (blogs, eRooms, Ning, Yahoo groups, etc.)

So how do you plan and manage migration? There is no exact prescription that will work perfectly for every org in every scenario. There are way too many variables involved.

You are implementing a new system, introducing it to new users, adding new capabilities, granting new rights, and giving new responsibilities. The complexity of the original system combined with the complexity of the new system will determine the complexity of the migration.

## Inventory, Assess, Enhance, Publish

Content migrations always start with a conversation.

"We need to determine what is going to be migrated to SharePoint. Has anyone completed an inventory of the content?"

"Yep. We have 350GB worth of files on the P:\ drive. We need to migrate it all into SharePoint. Our file share has been in use for more than 10 years. We just want to replicate in SharePoint what we have today."

**Do not replicate what you are doing today just because that's the way you've always been doing it.**

It is extremely rare to migrate everything you have, exactly as it exists today, into SharePoint. So how do you decide what content to migrate? How do you execute the migration? What should be automated? What should be manual? Here is a simple four-step approach for your content migration.

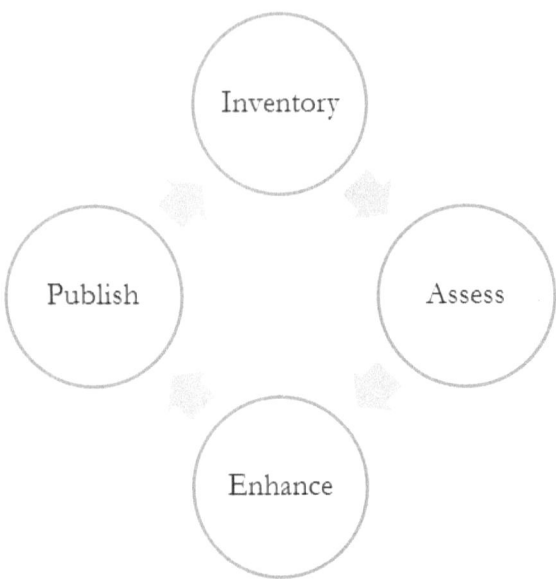

## Inventory

A successful content migration strategy should begin with determining what content you *have today*, as well as what content you *will have, want to have,* and *need to have.* Remember you are building a solution and not just implementing SharePoint. The inventory step is often performed poorly and sometimes not at all.

It is easy to determine what you have. If you are migrating file shares, analyze the file directory structure. If you have an existing CMS product or even a static website, analyze the pages. If you have a large amount of pages or files, there are utilities which can count, categorize, and index the content. You can even manually determine your inventory using a spreadsheet, a Word Document, an email, or a SharePoint List.

It's important to determine what content you *will have* in the new system for a variety of reasons.

➢ Determine your Information Architecture and Navigational elements based on the system you *will have* in place.

➢ Determine the Taxonomy based on the system you *will have* in place.

➢ Determine the user interface based on the system you *will have* in place.

➢ Determine what content you will NOT migrate based on the system you *will have* in place.

Determine what content you will *not* migrate. Do not migrate all content – you don't need to. Some of your users will tell you to migrate everything. It is extremely rare that you actually need to migrate everything.

Don't be afraid. Just because you don't migrate everything into SharePoint doesn't mean you can't access the content left behind. SharePoint Search can 'crawl' other applications, file shares, and websites. Allow your users to search for and find content which was not migrated.

Do not allow your users to continue using the old systems. Put the file share or the old copy of the website in read-only mode. Do not allow any further contributions or updates to that data in the original system. Allow it to be searched for historical purposes but do not continue to embrace or support it. Shun on!

## Assess

Once you have an inventory of current content and an idea of the content you will have, you can begin the content assessment.

If you are building a public-facing website or a volunteer training site, you can clearly see what you have, and what still needs to be developed. Use this opportunity wisely. Make assignments to have content owners evaluate the content. What's missing? How is the metadata? How is the organization? Where does the content fit into the IA? Does the content need edits?

After the assessment, you can perform a test migration of some or all of the content. You can see how it will look, work, and behave in the new SharePoint environment.

## Enhance

You are now educated on your content. You know what you have. You know what's missing. You know what the metadata *was*, if it existed at all. You know what the metadata should be in the new SharePoint environment. It's time to bridge the gap.

Focus on enhancing the content. Apply the appropriate Tags and metadata. Fill in the gaps. Update the Information Architecture. Add the missing content.

Rewrite the important content. If the new SharePoint Site you're building is public-facing or member-facing, this is a good time to spend considerable effort on the most popular Pages of your Site.

## Publish

Soft launch your new Site. A soft launch is similar to a beta test or preview. Some orgs choose to soft launch their SharePoint Site on a different URL while running their current environment. This affords the opportunity to perform a controlled release based on parameters you define.

You can roll out your Site to staff only. You can roll out your Site to a select group of members or volunteers and solicit feedback. You can share the updated Site with a select group of donors and request they fill out a survey for feedback.

You are in control of publishing and releasing your content, Site, and your platform – on your terms.

Now start the inventory, assessment, enhancement and publishing cycle *again*. And again. And again. Run through the cycle as many times as necessary. Feel free to perform the same cycles again *after* launch.

You do not have to launch all initiatives and solutions on SharePoint at the same time. Choose teams, projects, websites, and solutions, and deploy SharePoint using an iterative model as it makes sense for your org.

Finally, understand that SharePoint is a strategic business platform. Please don't just install it and hope for the best.

This is worth repeating in bold:

**SharePoint is a strategic business platform.**

Don't be intimidated by this. If you are using an AMS or CRM package, then you already have strategic *software*. While these are similar, they are not business *platforms*.

## Summary

Identify clear **business objectives** and problems to be solved. Determine if SharePoint is the *right* technology to satisfy your objectives.

Don't try to accomplish everything at once. Build a successful foundation and grow from there. Choose initial projects with high impact and visibility. Determine specific ROI goals and success metrics so you can gauge progress.

Make sure to consider the "human" aspect. Implementing a new solution impacts people and how they work. Take the time to understand how your people operate, and plan your new solution in a manner conducive to significantly improving their means of operating.

Get help! Hire it, rent it, or grow it. **Get help.** SharePoint is a large platform with a lot of capabilities. If you are not educated on the platform, you will end up building functions that already exist natively in SharePoint.

As with most platforms, there are multiple ways to do almost anything – some of them are better than others. That's why Best Practices exist.

# Governance

SharePoint is destined for failure without a Governance Plan. If you wish to personally guarantee the failure of your solution, skip this chapter now. Got your attention? Good.

Governance Planning is the most commonly overlooked step by orgs. It is important to establish a solid Governance Plan. Failure to do so can be linked to many failed SharePoint solutions.

The Governance Plan determines who does what, how they do it, and where it's done. What are the rules? Who gets to make the rules? Who enforces the rules?

The Governance Plan is a guideline covering administration, maintenance, and support of *your* SharePoint environments. It identifies lines of ownership for both business and technical teams, and defines who is responsible for what areas of the system. Furthermore, it establishes rules for appropriate usage of the SharePoint environments.

Your Governance Plan ensures the solution is used and managed in a controlled and consistent manner. Frankly, your Governance Plan is in place to prevent SharePoint from becoming unmanageable. A successful plan includes both a strategic, business-minded body to craft rules and procedures, and a tactical, technically-competent team to manage the routine operational tasks which keep the solution online.

Developing a Governance Plan does not need to be a massive undertaking, but adequate time needs to be allocated to this task. You can expect this to take between a couple of days and a couple of weeks to fully develop a comprehensive Governance Plan. Of course, it depends on the size and complexity of your solution and environment.

Why would you commit so much time to the Governance Plan? Without a documented plan, your SharePoint solution is at risk for becoming the Wild West. With no rules or guidance to follow, the only logical conclusion is chaos. Chaos, by definition, is impossible to manage.

Who will have permissions to create new Workspaces and Sites? How long are backups retained? How quickly should backups be available in case of catastrophic failure? How do you handle detractors such as negative comments or org bashing? These are just some of the questions your Governance Plan should answer.

Your Governance Plan will vary slightly depending on the solution being implemented and other factors related to your org. You do not have to write a complex Governance Plan from scratch.

Governance is a hot topic and is not specific to SharePoint environments. There are thousands of great resources online about Governance Plans. One of our favorites is specific to SharePoint and can be found on TechNet under "Governance Resource Center."

Your SharePoint Governance Plan should at a minimum include Business Objectives, Technical Requirements, Team Roles, Topology, Policies, and Training.

# Org Business Objectives

The name says it all! Identify and *document* the specific objectives and requirements the SharePoint solution is expected to satisfy. It may be easier to start with a high level business need and keep adding to it until the entire scene has been painted.

The Business Objectives section might start with something like "Our org has identified a need to improve collaboration. We feel that the best way to accomplish this is to provide employees with document management tools and improve the overall findability of our content and assets with a highly usable search application."

Expand the objective to include the entire business need and associated solution vision.

"Our org has identified a need to improve collaboration between departments. SharePoint will be used to provide employees with web-based document storage, document management and versioning tools, and team- and department-based workspaces. Employees will receive SharePoint training to make better use of the available tools to foster communication and improve document-based collaboration. SharePoint Search will be utilized to improve the overall findability of our org content and assets stored within SharePoint and on our existing file shares."

Remember to capture, clarify, and confirm your business objectives. This section is not technical in nature and should be reviewed and approved by the stakeholders.

## Technical Requirements

Unlike the Org Business Objectives, this section *is* technical in nature. Technical Requirements are all about the nuts and bolts of the solution, but only from a "must-haves" perspective.

For example, here are some examples of technical "must-haves" that should be considered within your Technical Requirements:

➤ **Planned Downtime**. A two-hour maintenance window for planned maintenance every Saturday beginning at 5:00AM EST.

➤ **Capacity Planning**. Hardware needs to scale and support the growth of the org. It needs to support 200GB of document storage at launch and scale to 600GB at 12 months. It must support 15,000 users for the first year, and it is expected to grow to 75,000 users at 24 months.

➤ **Disaster Recovery**. This environment must have a tested disaster recovery environment setup. SQL Server replication to our disaster recovery rack will suffice.

➤ **Availability**. Must be fault tolerant with load balanced web front ends, dedicated application server, and two-node clustered SQL Server. Availability target must be 99.9% or better.

➢ **Support calls**. Help desk calls should be received and attended within a maximum of 15-minute hold without a prior "high call volume" notification to the caller.

➢ **Audits**. Auditing to capture Site delete events should be in place from launch.

## Deployment Team Roles

Who's doing what? Do you need a RACI chart defining which individuals or roles are Responsible, Accountable, Consulted, and Informed? This is an important part of your playbook. It is important to document which roles are responsible for which activities. Without it, you run a high risk of experiencing diffusion of responsibility.

Please keep in mind that simply saying one person is "in charge of SharePoint" is more than just laziness – it's a recipe for disaster!

Your org may very well have your SharePoint "Go-To" person. The "Go-To" person should certainly play a vital role in your SharePoint planning and deployment. If you place the entire burden on one person's shoulders, you will have created a single point of failure and placed your solution in jeopardy. You will have a better solution if you enroll multiple people, identify their individual strengths, and request active and focused participation. SharePoint is a *team solution*. Use your team to construct your solution.

Roles will vary widely based on the size of your organization and on your specific SharePoint deployment. At a minimum, you need to account for the following Roles:

➤ **SharePoint Solution Architect.** Person or people responsible for initial planning of the entire solution, as well as for overseeing the proper execution during implementation and deployment. Needs a solid understanding of the business objectives, and must have the knowledge to satisfy these requirements using native SharePoint components, third-party add-ons, and custom development as necessary. Should be capable of interfacing with both business users and IT. Responsible for writing the technical specifications of the solution, and ensuring they are followed accordingly. This role can be outsourced.

➤ **SharePoint Developer.** The person or people responsible for writing custom code as prescribed by the SharePoint Architect. This should only happen after the Solution Architect has exhausted all other avenues of satisfying must-have functionality using native SharePoint components and existing third-party add-ons. This role can be outsourced.

➤ **SharePoint Administrator.** Person or people with Site Collection Administrator permissions; and responsible for administrative tasks such as ongoing maintenance, Search, Site procurement, Security, Templates, recovering deleted items from the Recycle Bin and managing the metadata and taxonomy configuration. *Not* responsible for architecting new solutions or writing code. Should interface very well with business users as well as IT, and understand when to call in the Solution Architect. If you have a Go-To SharePoint person, this would be the role he or she should belong in. This role can be outsourced.

➢ **SharePoint Support or SharePoint Governor.** Person or people responsible for helping business users overcome problems they might encounter. Must have a good understanding of the native capabilities of SharePoint from an end-user perspective. Needs to interface well with business users. Requires a level of patience and understanding usually possessed only by mothers. This role can be outsourced.

➢ **SharePoint Business Champion or Evangelist.** Person or people responsible for understanding their specific business unit's day-to-day activities, objectives, and inner-workings. The ability to recognize how SharePoint can be used to improve processes and efficiencies is a trait of this role. Lastly, having a positive outlook in general is a plus because they are the people advocating for the solution. Responsibilities include ensuring that their department understands the benefits of using SharePoint and serving as a liaison between the department and solution stakeholders in order to properly evolve the solution. This role can NOT be outsourced.

# SharePoint Topology

SharePoint farms come in all shapes and sizes. The Governance Plan will detail your specific farm layout (topology). Topologies range from single server to federated topologies with multiple farms being joined together. When deciding on a topology, be sure to document the layout, including any notes detailing what led to your decision.

Selecting the appropriate topology is a function of the SharePoint Architect role, but here are some sample scenarios.

**Standalone: SharePoint and SQL on a single server**

**Small Farm: SQL Server with one, two, or three SharePoint 2010 Servers**

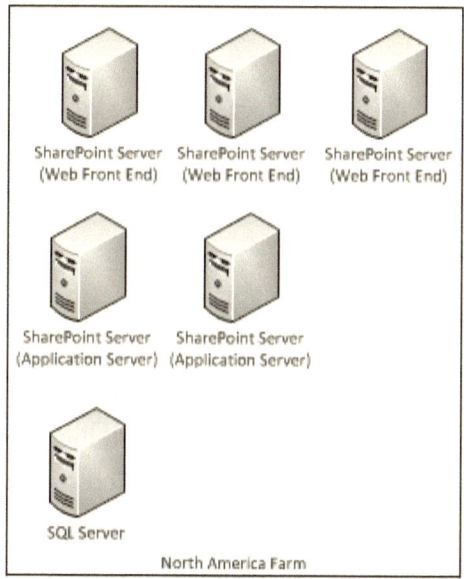

**Medium Farm: SQL Servers with four or more SharePoint 2010 Servers**

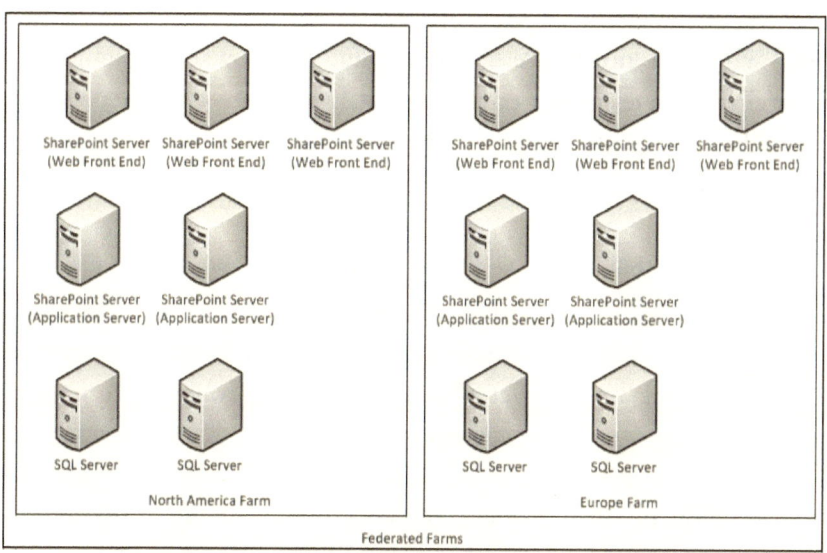

**Multiple Farms working together in Large or Federated Farms**

# Policies

This is the section of your Governance Plan where the rubber really meets the road. For obvious reasons, careful planning and consideration should go into your policies. You may need more policies than identified here.

## Customization Policy

The first bullet in this section should describe what your org considers a customization. It should describe the entire process from start to finish, particularly of how customizations shall be requested, approved, implemented, and all associated roles.

Typically, customizations are considered to be any third-party SharePoint add-ons or custom code (solutions, features, controls, etc.) which are not native to SharePoint. In-browser configuration, SharePoint Designer configuration, and everything else is considered configuration changes or native SharePoint functionality.

It is unlikely that your users will know exactly what to consider a "customization." Your policy needs to account for requests which may end up being "configuration changes" and not customizations. Your Customization Policy should include the following questions as part of your change management:

> ➤ How do users request customizations? Online form with workflow? Email? Both?

➢ What role is responsible for reviewing customization requests?

➢ What is an acceptable time lapse until the user receives a response?

➢ If it is determined that a request is actually a configuration change, what role approves this change?

➢ What role is responsible for funding customization efforts?

➢ What role is responsible for funding configuration efforts?

➢ How are customization requests tracked and communicated?

➢ Is the customization localized to a single Site, or is the customization useful across the org?

➢ What role is responsible to capture, clarify, and confirm the actual business objectives?

➢ How are customizations tested prior to being deployed on the Production servers?

**Detractor Policy**

Due to the social nature of the SharePoint My Sites, many orgs are paralyzed with fear when thinking of it. This is unfortunate because the concepts born out of social networking actually enhance and facilitate collaboration. We have found that adding a Detractors Policy to the Governance Plan instantly relaxes often unjustified concerns about social features.

The Detractors Policy of your Governance Plan can be a simple table with the following column headings:

➢ What type of Detractor?
   Example:  Legitimate complainer.

➢ Why they make trouble.
   Example:  Needs help with or wants to warn others.

➢ How to recognize Detractor?
   Example:  Raises legitimate issue and may use strong language but seems open to reason.

➢ What is the corrective action?
   Example:  Solve problem, provide education, or explain policies.  Explain publicly or add to FAQ if possible.

You will be surprised how quickly fears related to the What-Ifs go away when they are written down and accounted for!  More on What-Ifs later.

## Site Provisioning Policy

How are new Sites requested?  Who can request a new Site?  What Workflow is required?  What role approves the request?  Where does the new Site get created?  What about unused Sites? When are Sites archived? Deleted?

## Site Management and Security Model Policy

What roles are responsible for which Sites? What permissions are associated with which roles? What are the Farm Service Accounts being used and the associated passwords? Who are the Site Collection Administrators? Who are the Site Administrators? Who provides backups to Administrators?

## Retention Policy

How long do we keep content? What do we do with content we consider old? Archive it? Remove it? Permanently delete it? Request the Author to update it?

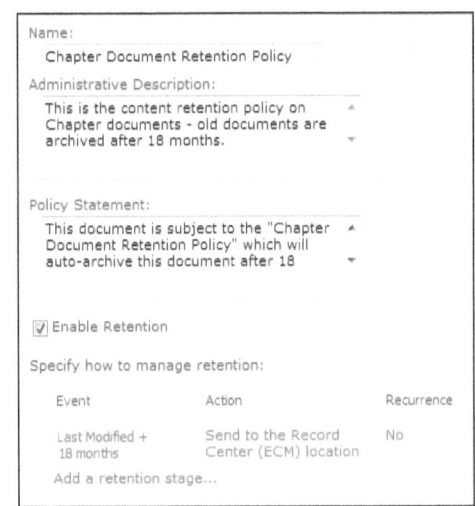

**Create New Retention Policy**

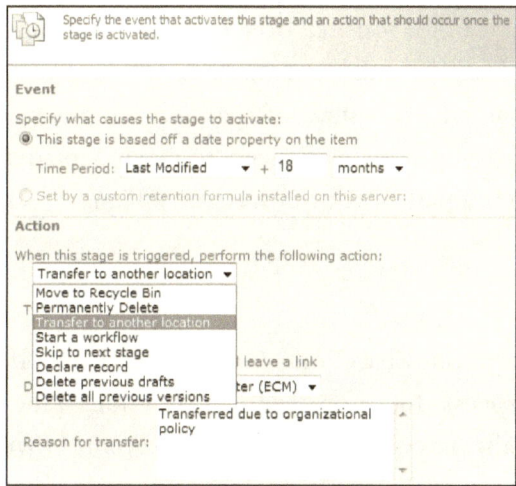

**Specify Document Retention Action**

# Training

Do not overlook training. Your Governance Plan should detail initial training, ongoing training, and training levels that are audience specific. Training for administrators is different than training for business users. Training for chapter leaders is different than for volunteers.

Determine each of the different groups to receive training and the level of training required. Determine the type of training required for each group as well. IT Pros and technical administrators are usually fine with written training. Volunteers and members usually find webinar or video-based training more effective.

Don't stop with training at launch. Ensure your org supports ongoing training options for new hires, community leaders, business users, executives, and members.

Your training can be onsite, offsite, video, online, live webinar, recorded webinar, three days, or three-minute snippets that describe specific actions and activities. Regardless of the type of training that works for your org, you need to have a plan for it. Your Training Plan is a part of your Governance Plan.

## Summary

Do not neglect your SharePoint Governance Plan. It will not end well. This process does not need to take a long time to complete, but it is vitally important. Your SharePoint Governance Plan should, at a minimum, include the following sections:

Your **Business Objectives** define the high level objectives which the solution is expected to satisfy. Your **Technical Requirements** define the technical components of the solution, including integration points with external Line of Business (LOB) systems like your AMS, CRM, and all other non-SharePoint data sources.

Your **Deployment Team Roles** define who is responsible for what. Your **SharePoint Topology** defines your SharePoint network and server farm architecture, including number of servers, server roles, specifications, and other relevant information.

Your **Governance Plan Policies** define your business rules which describe how you handle events such as procuring new Sites.

> ➤ Your **Customization Policy** specifies the rules on how third-party products and custom components are identified, tested, and ultimately deployed to the production environment.

> ➤ Your **Detractors Policy** provides guidance in undesirable situations such as members saying less than flattering things about your org or solution(s) undertaken.

> ➤ Your **Site Management and Security Policy** specifies ongoing Site and Subsite management and the responsible roles.

> ➤ Your **Retention Policy** defines how long content remains until considered unnecessary, and what to do with it.

Finally, your **Training Plan** outlines your official launch, as well as the conduct of ongoing and refresher training with respect to the diverse audiences and their existing workloads.

# User Adoption: A Paradigm Shift

For many orgs, user adoption is the most challenging aspect of SharePoint. Many SharePoint solutions are less about technology change and more about the paradigm shift in user behavior. The money invested and your hard work, the planning, and the implementation are of little consequence without user adoption. You do not want your solution to go down in history as a failure.

User adoption is a critical component of any SharePoint implementation, and should be considered a high priority objective. Ensure your SharePoint solution is utilized by identifying and executing a workable user adoption strategy.

Every org has a slightly different user adoption strategy simply because all orgs are different. Some orgs have an old-school culture where anything related to technology and computers is just difficult. At the other end of the spectrum, some orgs take great pride in utilizing cutting edge technology whenever possible. Most orgs fall somewhere in the middle.

Most orgs consist of staff, members, and supporters of all ages, backgrounds, and interests with a wide range of technical comfort levels. The common denominator for all of these people is time or rather, the *lack* of time.

No one wants to waste time trying to figure things out. It is important to make sure any new solution is perceived as an enhancement for everyone and not just some IT project. Fantastic user adoption happens through strategic planning, user involvement, and active participation.

## User Adoption Strategy

User adoption does not happen by accident. It requires thoughtful consideration. Even if your SharePoint solution makes everything easier for all users, that alone will not motivate users to use *any* new system. How many times have your users heard the new solution will make their life easier?

Give your users a sense of ownership through participation and involvement. You are building solution ambassadors. Iteratively roll out new exciting features and capabilities on a regular basis. Users need a positive first impression, and they need education on the SharePoint solution. You need a strategy to accomplish all of this.

Keep in mind we encourage you to add your own perspective to these ideas. You know your org better than we do. These are just some things we've seen help orgs achieve successful user adoption.

## Involvement and Participation

Involvement is not the same as participation with regard to user adoption. Involvement means you're connected to the solution in some way, and that can sometimes be a stretch. "Jim from Accounting" might be indirectly involved with the SharePoint solution simply because he uses a SharePoint Document Library to store spreadsheets. This is not the level of involvement necessary, and this does not resemble successful user adoption.

Users should participate early in the solution business objectives stage. Don't discuss the technical requirements at this early stage. Don't mention SharePoint or any technology terms.

Initially, your users should be asked to explain how they currently do things and provide any ideas for improvements. Encourage them to express opinions regarding ways to increase efficiency, improve processes, reduce mundane and redundant tasks, etc.

How quickly can they find what they are looking for? How often are they asked the exact, same question? What processes should be automated? What reports, documents, spreadsheets, or forms do they use on a regular basis? What ideas do they have to help with their own jobs? What about the other people they are working with or for?

Ask your users these types of questions and you can turn passive involvement into active participation. Let your users know that all of their ideas are welcome, and that you also need help prioritizing these ideas.

Be sure to keep track of your findings as well as which individual or group came up with the idea. This will later come in handy when you publicly thank them for their active role in the solution requirements. Thank them for their thought leadership! If you do this with honest sincerity, users will beam with pride and be happy to actively utilize your new SharePoint solution. Often, these same users will become evangelists, spreading their excitement about the new solution and continually providing useful feedback and ideas.

## Planned Feature Rollouts

Another great way to achieve and sustain user adoption is to have a plan for rolling out new features. SharePoint is big. We have had great success by iteratively deploying features and capabilities. Begin with a smaller feature set or a smaller group of users. Plan, implement, assess, and then evaluate. Then do it again, with a wider audience. Start with a small team, committee, council, or department. Obtain feedback, modify the solution, and then roll it out wider.

People may seem to resist change on a large scale, but they do not mind small changes. Do not overwhelm your users (and yourself) by building a complete system and deploying hundreds of new processes and features users have to learn.

By actively involving users during the business objectives stage, you can quickly identify the "low hanging fruit." When you plan your SharePoint deployment, try to plan for at least one high priority feature from each group to help build your evangelists. Even if including a high-priority feature is simply not possible in this cycle, try and roll out two or more mid-priority items.

Even more importantly – **communicate** these decisions and actions. Users should understand what is happening, why it's happening, and when they can expect their personal objectives to be met. One of the questions that every one of your users will be asking is "What's in it for me?"

Develop a strategy and plan features to be rolled out on a scheduled basis. Some orgs add features and functionality every six months, while some add capabilities every couple of weeks.

Your implementation schedule will likely change as your solution progresses, but communicating a published plan goes a long way with user adoption. The process of releasing new functionality over a period of time decreases the learning curve, and creates an environment where the importance of the users is crystal clear.

We have never seen a solution fail due to over-communication.

## Ownership

Can you take pride in something without a sense of ownership? Your users need to have a sense of ownership in your SharePoint solution. We are not talking about security permissions, but rather something they can take credit for. They want something to call their own, and something they can be proud of.

You can easily promote ownership by implementing a feature a user recommended. It does not matter if that feature was going to be enabled anyway. What matters is a user can view their little piece of the SharePoint solution with pride. They now have a sense of ownership.

Be creative with your users. For example: create a new help section and give credit to "Betty from Membership" because she had concerns regarding usability. Give her credit for the fantastic idea of a "Help Section" for the new volunteers. Determine who is passionate and what they are passionate about. Harness your team's energy as part of the SharePoint solution.

However, resist adding things to your solution for the sole purpose of giving someone a sense of ownership. Allowing users to enjoy a sense of ownership can be achieved without diluting solution functionality. Without a sense of ownership, user adoption is at risk. Without user adoption, your solution will be left for dead.

## Ambassadors

The concept of having solution ambassadors might sound strange, but it's actually common with SharePoint. SharePoint can cover such vast amounts of feature real-estate; it's easy for SharePoint-based solutions to pick up fans. This may not happen without gentle nudging, but it is a critical component of your user adoption strategy.

Strike while the iron is hot! The best time to deputize a new ambassador is when they are singing songs of praise about a single part of the solution. Let them know you appreciate their positive approach. Candidates may include virtually anybody possessing the following traits: they have the desire to help others, they provide positive reinforcement, they look for and offer solutions, and they do not detract from others' user adoption. Beware the Detractors!

We've seen some interesting ways to encourage such behavior. Formally distinguish someone as an "Expert." They could be the expert in one area of passion, like the Business Intelligence Expert, Search Expert, or Collaboration Expert.

Another great way to encourage ambassadors and show your appreciation is to host an event. Invite only active participants who have demonstrated a high level of helpfulness. This is even more important when considering extranets where your members, volunteers, donors, affiliates, and supporters gather and collaborate. Often times, these are content-specific or industry-specific experts helping each other out, answering questions, blogging, commenting, etc. These are the extremely important users and your community leaders. They are your ambassadors.

## Bad first impressions

We've all heard you don't get a second chance at a first impression. When it comes to user adoption, truer words have never been spoken. We have been involved in plenty of cleanups and re-deployments over the years. Earning back user trust is about the hardest thing you will encounter with any solution, and SharePoint is no exception. When someone has a negative experience, they will recoil at the slightest hint of a problem. It takes time to earn back their trust.

What if it's already too late for a first impression? How do you perform a cleanup anyway? You find a problem, and you fix it!

Start small, and keep cleaning until you're done. You must maintain focus on the solution and constantly evolve the solution to ensure your users are getting what they need and want from it.

Do not get defensive during a cleanup. Don't point fingers. Your SharePoint solution may be sound and may have been implemented properly. Perhaps users don't understand how to use it. Maybe they were not properly trained or the training happened long ago, prior to going live. Whatever the circumstances, you are potentially walking into an emotionally charged situation and you need to be sensitive and diplomatic.

Don't refer to your solution as "SharePoint." You don't talk with users about Active Directory, Exchange, SQL or your AMS, do you? We walk into situations where SharePoint has been implemented poorly and people don't want to hear about how "SharePoint" will make things better *this time*. In fact, they may not want to hear anything about SharePoint at all. They want to do the talking, and they want to be heard.

This is your opportunity to engage your users and begin the process of getting buy-in. A good place to start is by listening to what they have to say and go back to gathering business objectives.

## Education

Proper education leads user adoption and will greatly enhance the user experience. Nobody wants to spend valuable time trying to figure out how to use a solution which is *supposed* to make everything easier. Education is important, and timing is everything. Audience specific education at the appropriate time will contribute to successful user adoption.

Training will be divided into *at least* two groups: the implementation team and the end users. The implementation team is responsible for the initial implementation of your SharePoint solution and may also be your ongoing SharePoint support team. The implementation team should receive broad and general SharePoint training prior to solution implementation.

On the other hand, your end users should receive solution-specific training, at most one day prior to launch. You may even provide training on the day of launch. This timing will help ensure that everything they learned is still fresh in their heads when they start using the solution.

## Audience-specific training

One class offered across the board won't cut it. Make sure each audience receives the appropriate level and amount of training. End user training on SharePoint can typically be broken down into two main categories based on your solution type: Content Authors and Power Users.

Content Author training is for users publishing content to your SharePoint Site. Content Author training covers the basics of authoring, reviewing, approving, and publishing content to the Site.

Power User training targets a select group and covers more advanced components such as creating Workflows, Lists, Libraries, Sites, Site Templates, and possibly SharePoint Designer.

Depending upon the size of your org and your commitment to SharePoint, you may also designate at least one staff person as your SharePoint Administrator. Ensure this person (or team) receives proper SharePoint Administration training in addition to all other training offered.

Do not cut corners when it comes to training. Splurge for the proper training and ensure the training includes solution-specific methodologies. Real-world examples should be used in training, and the examples should be applicable to the specific group being trained.

If possible, require training. Continuing education is something employees and members typically appreciate, and you should not experience much resistance. Ensure your training timeframe is flexible enough to accommodate everyone's schedule. Classes should be offered on two different days, allowing users to select one which best fits their heavy workload.

Throughout the year, offer periodic refresher courses. Encourage participation of those who have already attended. Require participation of those who have not yet attended. Appropriate SharePoint training will contribute to successful user adoption. Training will also help your organization run more effectively.

## Small wins

The initial implementation is most important, but it doesn't end there. By repeatedly implementing small changes and enhancing the SharePoint solution, you keep users engaged by providing new and better ways of doing things. You also improve your solution's sustainability. Continue gathering feedback and implementing requests which make sense according to your Governance Plan. In doing so, you will accumulate many "small wins" which help ensure your user adoption rate stays high.

Keep adding to your solution by continuously procuring new Sites, adding third-party solutions, and creating new dashboard Pages, Discussion Boards, Surveys, etc. Your wins do not need to be large enhancements or require significant customization.

Small wins just need to solve problems. This is another opportunity to promote ownership among users. You may even be able to turn more users into ambassadors! Implementing small wins encourages active participation.

## The Carrot

Let's consider the use of the "carrot" (positive) and the "stick" (negative) as incentives for increasing user adoption. The spirit of successful user adoption is of solution buy-in and mutual respect. The carrot approach allows you to achieve short-term wins as well as a long-term promise. The user adoption strategies discussed thus far have been in accordance with the carrot approach.

## The Stick

User adoption can be approached from a very different angle, a much darker approach with short-term promise for sure. Simply take the old, top-down tactic of dictating exactly how things are going to work in your org. Assimilate, or be destroyed!

This approach will not work at all for members, volunteers, or supporters, and at best will only provide the appearance of working with staff. The *do-things-this-way-because-I'm-the-boss* will only work if your employees are mindless order-takers. If this were in fact the case, they would likely not have been hired in the first place.

Your staff may start using the solution or appear to be using the solution, but this will be short-lived. While this approach to achieving user adoption may work in a military situation, it will undoubtedly prove less than ideal in your org. In the case of The Carrot vs. The Stick, it's easy to see the undisputed champion when it comes to achieving user adoption.

## Summary

Not everybody in your organization will be tripping over daisies with any new solution implementation. Many people will initially resist any change. You may not achieve 100% user adoption; but that is okay. We humans are fickle beings. There are often too many variables coming in to play affect our decisions at any given moment.

Build a user adoption strategy which will ultimately guarantee the overall success of your SharePoint solution. Use involvement and participation to develop active participants.

**Plan Feature Rollouts** and let everyone know what features are coming and when to expect them. Give your users a sense of **ownership** and pride. Create solution **ambassadors** through encouragement and gratitude. Make a good **first impression** – definitely don't screw this up. Not all training is created equal. Provide appropriate training to the respective audiences. **Education** is vitally important to the success of your SharePoint solution. Continue gathering feedback requests and implement appropriate changes through **small wins**.

# Taxonomy and Folksonomy

Taxonomy and Folksonomy are types of metadata fundamental to solid information architecture.

## Taxonomy

Taxonomy is a formal classification using a tiered term structure.

**Domain – Kingdom – Phylum – Class – Order – Family – Genus – Species**

You knew it at one time. You also learned another one: the Dewey Decimal Classification System. These are some of the most well-known classification systems on the planet. Dewey Decimal taxonomy has been used for more than 130 years and is still in use by more than 200,000 libraries worldwide. There's a reason – it makes sense. Taxonomy represents a structured system of classification, thus providing a unified vocabulary. Taxonomy is centrally managed and consistently applied to content.

## Folksonomy

Folksonomy, on the other hand, refers to categorization by the users. That's right, you can *crowdsource* part of your taxonomy and let your users determine how the content should be classified.

SharePoint 2010 provides this natively using Keywords which gives the power of tag-based classification to individual users. Users can tag content using any Keywords they wish.

They can use their own tags to describe a Page, video, document, image, or any other piece of content. Your user has the option to make each Keyword public or private. If the user selects to keep a Keyword private, only that specific user sees how they tagged content.

To manage all taxonomy and folksonomy capabilities, SharePoint 2010 introduces a new multi-faceted, tiered classification system across your entire SharePoint infrastructure called Managed Metadata, or Managed Metadata Services. Managed Metadata supports both a formal taxonomy and an informal folksonomy.

## Terms

Terms are the fundamental building blocks of the SharePoint 2010 taxonomy and folksonomy system. A Term is a word or phrase that can be associated with an Item in SharePoint. Terms are collectively stored in a database referred to as the Term Store.

SharePoint provides the tools for associating these words with any type of content. Users with Internet Explorer can even tag websites which are not even part of your SharePoint solution.

Terms are split into two types: *Managed Terms* which represent taxonomy and *Enterprise Keywords* which represent folksonomy. Managed Terms can be organized in a parent-child hierarchy. Terms may be predefined by entering your org's tags into the SharePoint Term Store management interface, or by uploading an Excel spreadsheet populated with your tags. Term Sets can even have specific managers which can add, update, and delete terms.

For example, your org may elect to have one person manage the Terms related to Government Affairs while different people manage the Terms related to medical conditions. Your org can structure the parent-child hierarchy using *your* information. The Term Set structure can be as simple or as complex as you need.

A word of caution: start simple. Do not make it cumbersome for your content authors to appropriately tag your content. Make it easy. We have seen orgs start with overly complicated taxonomy structures which are improperly used.

**A simple classification system correctly applied is infinitely more powerful than a complex system used improperly.**

Enterprise Keywords, on the other hand, are all stored in a single keyword set that does not support a hierarchal structure. Enterprise Keywords do not require specific permissions to manage. You can allow any user to add Keywords. Members,

Volunteers, Donors, Board Members, Chapter Leaders, Registered Users, or anyone you wish.

## Benefits of Classification

Classification allows content to be related to similar content. There are many websites which display "Related Articles", "Related Events" or "Other Products You Might Like" – all based on the classification of the content being viewed. Once your content has been tagged (classified) properly, SharePoint can easily display other similarly tagged pieces of content.

Classification also allows you to relate content to users. Users can enjoy a highly personalized experience when logged into your Site. For example, users may indicate an interest in Government Affairs within their profile. Content may also be tagged as relating to Government Affairs.

SharePoint can use this information to display content related to Government Affairs to this user on any Page you wish. You can configure Web Parts to show other articles, upcoming events, products, or any other content that has been tagged with Government Affairs.

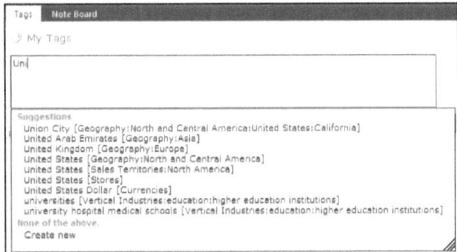

**Suggestions are provided when adding tags**

Classification also provides the ability to sort and filter based on how content has been tagged. If users are uploading documents into your SharePoint intranet and are appropriately tagging the content as they upload, it becomes very easy to apply a filter and show all documents in a library with a certain tag.

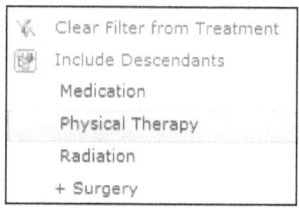

**Apply filter**

Assuming users are tagging content, it's easy to predefine List Views that show only Items that have been tagged with certain Keywords or Terms.

Let's assume that we have an association of automobile owners. Our formal taxonomy might have a Term Set which specifically describes various car components: safety, price, rating, manufacturer, and color. As staff create and upload documents to the internal research Document Library, these documents would be tagged with the various topics. A View that shows only documents which have been tagged as "safety" makes life easier for anyone looking for documents related to auto safety.

You have spent and still spend a lot of time trying to organize the content of your website into logical buckets. Afterwards, you put a nice navigation bar in place to provide your Site users with a very simple and intuitive way to go find content in your Site. Everyone can now find anything they want anywhere in your Site, right? If so, congratulations! You have a perfect Information Architecture and a perfect navigation structure that needs no further explanation or clarification! You have achieved what no one else ever has! It's time to retire!

If you are like the rest of us, you could use additional ways for users to find the information they need when they need it. You did put the navigation in place. Wouldn't it be nice to have a way for users to actually navigate the content using the new taxonomy you have in place? SharePoint 2010 offers Managed Metadata features which make finding any needed content even easier.

Search refinements are covered in greater detail in the Search chapter, just know SharePoint 2010 provides Term Filtering for both Managed Terms and Enterprise Keywords on search results. This works off the shelf with no required customization.

**Search Results Page**

Managed Metadata is associated with content through the use of Site Columns. This means it's very easy to leverage the Managed

Metadata using any of the native capabilities in SharePoint, such as the Content Query Web Part (CQWP).

The CQWP is one of the Swiss Army Web Parts. You can accomplish many content aggregation tasks with just this single Web Part.

The CQWP allows you to use Managed Metadata fields to create very Amazon.com-like behavior within your Pages. If you are looking at an Article Page related to automobile safety, you can use the CQWP to show "Other pages related to Auto Safety" or "Upcoming Events related to Auto Safety."

## Personalization

Every one of us likes to be treated special. Dale Carnegie wrote in 1936, "Remember that a person's name is to that person the sweetest and most important sound in any language."

That has not changed. Even in the language of the web, we like our content served up specifically for us. We don't want to wade through hundreds of links. If we express what we're interested in, we expect that information to be used for providing us relevant information.

Using the social features in SharePoint 2010, users can specify tags they are interested in. These tags may be Managed Terms (taxonomy) or Enterprise Keywords (folksonomy). Either way, SharePoint will serve up content tagged with terms users are interested in on their Newsfeed. This is individual personalization based on Keywords!

Personalization can also be accomplished using SharePoint Audiences. Audiences are groups of users you have created based on similar attributes.

For example, you can create an Audience called "Volunteers Interested in Auto Safety." Users in this SharePoint Audience have at some point indicated "Auto Safety" as an interest within their User Profile.

The ability to target content towards a specific Audience is available in many SharePoint Web Parts. This level of personalization is quickly becoming the norm on websites, and can only fully be truly successful and relevant after a carefully planned and managed taxonomy structure is in place.

## Summary

Taxonomy is a fundamental Information Architecture building block which empowers you to better organize and present your content. Taxonomy is simply **classification of your content.** It is extremely useful for the following reasons:

➢ Relating content to other pieces of content.
➢ Relating content to people (personalization).
➢ Aggregating content from multiple locations into a single display.
➢ Improving search.

**Taxonomy** is the formal, hierarchical structure of tags which are usually managed by staff. **Folksonomy** is similar to taxonomy, but users create the tags. Members, Volunteers, Donors, Board

Members, Chapter Leaders, Registered Users, or anyone you allow can add tags to your folksonomy. SharePoint offers both, and both are very important.

In SharePoint 2010, Terms are your taxonomy, and Keywords are your folksonomy.

**Personalization** can also be achieved using SharePoint Audiences. Audiences are logical groups of users that you define with similar attributes.

# SharePoint Owner's Manual

SharePoint makes it easy to keep a nice clean house, but there are a few things beyond regular maintenance which should receive proper attention. The SharePoint Recycle Bin can quickly transform you into a card carrying hero. Usage Audits can reveal under-utilized areas as candidates for archival or removal. Information Management Policies may be used to automate content policies in your org. Facilitate content organization by properly configuring Document Libraries.

## Document Library Tips

Document Libraries have so much flexibility it can be difficult for an org to define exactly how they should be used. Since planning is critical, here are some tips which will have a positive impact on your collaborative environment.

### Require Check Out

Use the Require Check Out option on your Document Libraries. This is especially important in the Document Libraries where multiple people have permissions to modify the files. Require Check Out forces users to Check Out any file before making changes and saving it back into the Document Library. This prevents multiple authors from editing the document simultaneously. There are times you may elect to disable Require Check Out – make that the *exception* and not the rule. The entire concept of Check Out may be new for many users. Before implementing anything related to Check Out, make sure users understand how (and what it means) to Check In, Check Out, and Discard Check Out.

We're trying to focus on SharePoint, but know that Microsoft Office 2010 introduces simultaneous document authoring or co-authoring – allowing multiple authors to edit the *same* document at the exact same moment. Just because the technology is capable does not mean your users are ready.

The View below displays four columns:

- ➢ Type (icon linked to document)
- ➢ Name (linked to document with edit menu)
- ➢ Modified
- ➢ Checked Out To

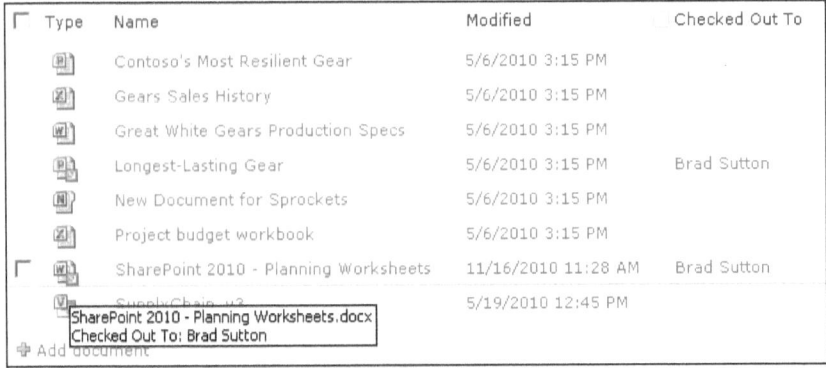

| Type | Name | Modified | Checked Out To |
|---|---|---|---|
| | Contoso's Most Resilient Gear | 5/6/2010 3:15 PM | |
| | Gears Sales History | 5/6/2010 3:15 PM | |
| | Great White Gears Production Specs | 5/6/2010 3:15 PM | |
| | Longest-Lasting Gear | 5/6/2010 3:15 PM | Brad Sutton |
| | New Document for Sprockets | 5/6/2010 3:15 PM | |
| | Project budget workbook | 5/6/2010 3:15 PM | |
| | SharePoint 2010 - Planning Worksheets | 11/16/2010 11:28 AM | Brad Sutton |
| | SupplyChain v3 | 5/19/2010 12:45 PM | |

SharePoint 2010 - Planning Worksheets.docx
Checked Out To: Brad Sutton

⊕ Add document

**Document Library View**

This View shows the Checked Out files in three ways:

> ➤ The icon changes to display a small green arrow indicating Check Out.

> ➤ When a user hovers over the icon, a dialog will appear showing the Document Name and Checked Out To.

> ➤ The Checked Out To column indicates the file is Checked Out by showing a user's name.

It's useful to add the Checked Out By Column to the default View of the Document Library to make it clear who has the file checked out.

Ensure someone on the working team (other than IT) has the Permission to Override Check Out. You don't want to bother the IT team with non-IT tasks just because someone forgets to Check In an Item before going on vacation!

**Versioning**

Use Document Version History capabilities. It really is that simple: use Versioning.

When using Versioning, only use Minor Versions when you have a need to hide Draft Versions. Set version retention limits which strike a realistic balance between usefulness and the amount of available database space.

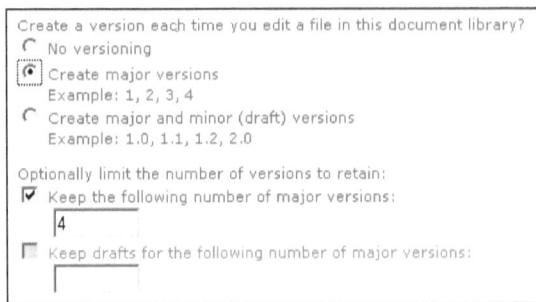

**Versioning**

## Views

Configure Views to help users quickly find what they are looking for regardless of the number of files contained in the Document Library.

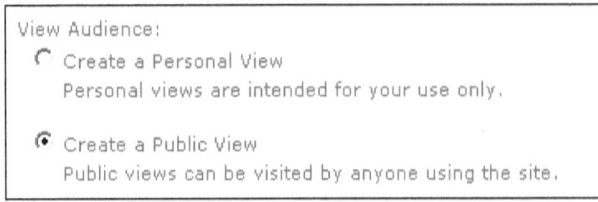

**Create a Public View**

Users should be trained to create and utilize Personal Views to maximize effectiveness of Lists and Libraries while minimizing user interface clutter.

## Structure

Do not replicate your shared drive hierarchy in SharePoint. SharePoint is more powerful than a drive share. Do not configure SharePoint as you did with your file share just because that's the way things have "always been done." Use SharePoint for more than just document storage.

Folders are safe and easy. People understand using Folders. The concept of using computerized folders to organize files logically has been used for more than 50 years. Folders do have their place.

**Don't go crazy creating Folders.**

Folders can be used to control permissions on a group of Files contained within a Document Library, but use Folders sparingly. Use metadata instead.

Metadata can be used to group files together in Views. This can give the appearance of Folders. This is a powerful way to facilitate user adoption. Using metadata instead of Folders is largely accepted as a best practice.

Finally, integrate your SharePoint metadata (Columns and Site Columns) directly into Microsoft Word 2007 or 2010 using Quick Parts to link content from your document to SharePoint metadata.

# Content Types

A Content Type is a reusable collection of metadata, which SharePoint refers to as Columns. A Content Type may have associated workflows, behaviors, and other settings for use as Items or documents in Lists or Document Libraries. Content Types provide a powerful centralized tool to manage the structure of information in a reusable way.

Use Content Types for commonly used information and file templates, and associate these Content Types with your Document Libraries. Document-based Content Types allow you to upload and associate the template file into the Content Type.

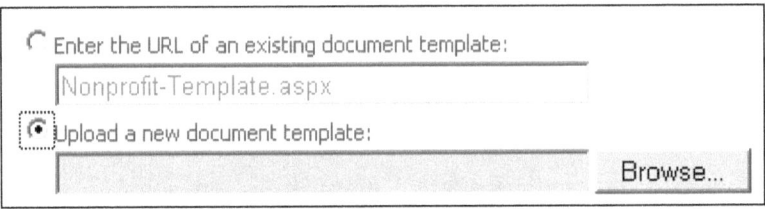

**Associate Template with Content Type**

When a user clicks the "New" button on the Library, they can choose the appropriate Content Type based upon the correct template.

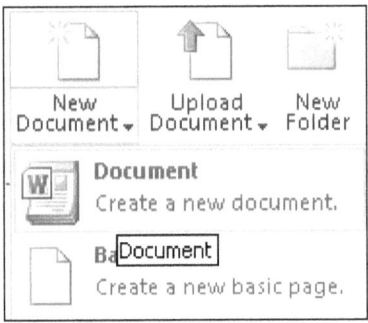

**Create New Document**

When a user starts a new document using the New Document button in a Document Library, that Document Library will be the default location when saving the document. If a document is started directly in Word, the user will need to navigate to the appropriate Document Library using the Save As dialog.

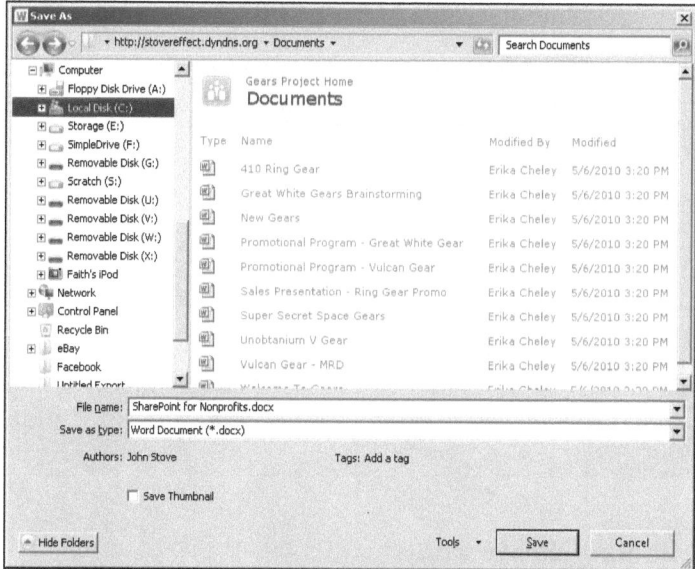

**Save to SharePoint Document Library directly from Word**

## Recycle Bin

Membership directors and executives at orgs often express concern about giving members and volunteers tools and permissions to work on content in a full collaborative model. Distributed volunteers don't have access to the same training as staff, and they may not have a full understanding of the capabilities they have been given. What if they change a document? What if they *delete* something?

The SharePoint Recycle Bin is your safety net. It catches the deleted documents, Items, Lists, Folders, and files. When an *authorized* user elects to delete an Item, SharePoint prompts the user with a familiar message: "Are you sure?"

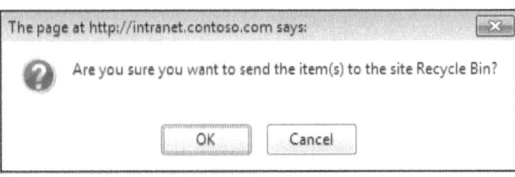

**Confirm Delete**

The SharePoint Recycle Bin has two stages, cleverly named Stage One and Stage Two. Stage One is located at the Site (or Subsite) level and is accessible to users with Contribute, Design, or Full Control permissions. The Stage Two Recycle Bin is at the Site Collection level (root) and is only available to Site Collection Administrators.

## How the Recycle Bin works

Deleted Items go to the Stage One Recycle Bin in the Site the Item was deleted. After a pre-determined time period (default is 30 days), the Item is sent to the Stage Two Recycle Bin. This second stage keeps the Item until the Stage Two Recycle Bin reaches its storage capacity limit, at which point the oldest Items are deleted.

You can control how much disk space is available to the Stage Two Recycle Bin at the Web Application level (Central Administration Site). The Recycle Bin storage space does not count toward the Site Quota (the allocated storage space). The specified size does, in fact, increase the total size of the actual SQL Content Database for that Site. It is considered a best practice to express this value as a percentage of the Site Quota allocated.

Items cannot be restored over an existing Item with the same name. This conflict is handled by Versioning. The Recycle Bin does not store deleted Versions. Items in the Stage Two Recycle Bin can only be restored by a Site Collection Administrator. Turning off the Recycle Bin will *permanently delete* all Items it contains at the time. Do not turn off the Recycle Bin without thoughtful consideration. Better yet, do not turn off the Recycle Bin.

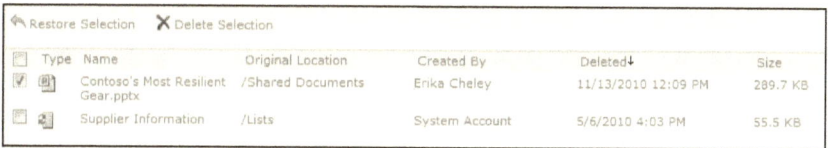

**Restore from Stage One Recycle Bin**

Items from either stage of the SharePoint Recycle Bin can easily be restored by authorized users.

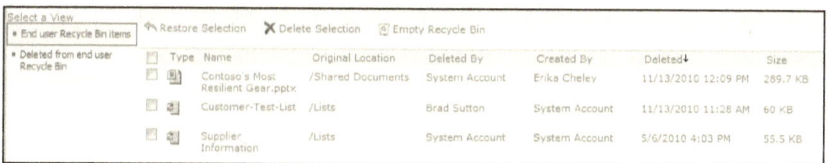

**Stage Two Recycle Bin**

# Site Usage

SharePoint can bring complete transparency to an org. The auditing and reporting features in SharePoint provide various windows to see what's really happening in your org. The Site Usage Reporting capabilities provide a way to review general web analytics information. There are also Search Usage reports which show what users are *looking for and clicking on* as well as what they are *looking for and not finding.*

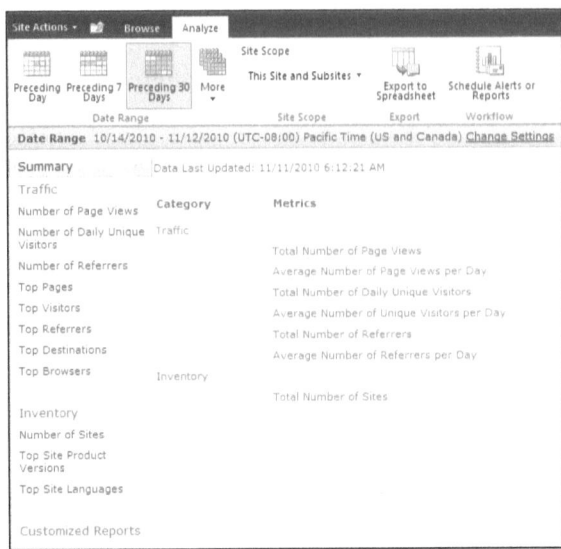

**Site Usage Summary**

Search Usage provides insights which are incredibly useful both inside and outside the org. When designing the Information Architecture and related navigation, orgs put a great deal of effort in trying to determine what users will want when they come to the site. The Search Usage reports show us *exactly* what the users are actually looking for. Maybe even more important to an org is the Search Usage report showing what they are looking for and *not finding*.

There could be hot new topics or key legislation which you don't have available on your website —maybe you should! There could be a lot of searches for content which IS on your website, but users aren't finding due to terminology discrepancies.

Search Usage reports are a great way to stay in touch with how people are actually using your site. Don't just peruse the Search

Usage reports - *use* this information to assist with the management of your site. Give your members what they are looking for.

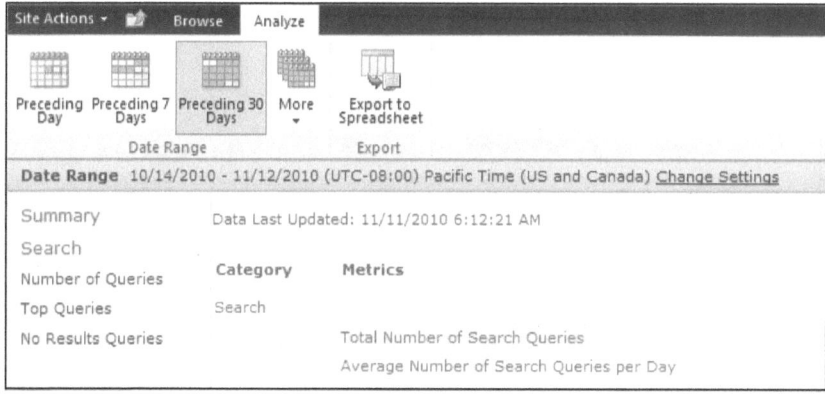

**Search Usage Reports**

SharePoint analytics are included, but you can also use third-party web analytics packages such as Google Analytics (which is free), Adobe Omniture, WebTrends, or any other package to provide additional capabilities to the reporting available with SharePoint.

## Audit Log Reports

Everyone loves reports. What if you want reports which are more specific to content activities or information management? Who is downloading, updating, or deleting a particular file? Why did a document disappear and then reappear later? Enter Custom Audit Log Reports.

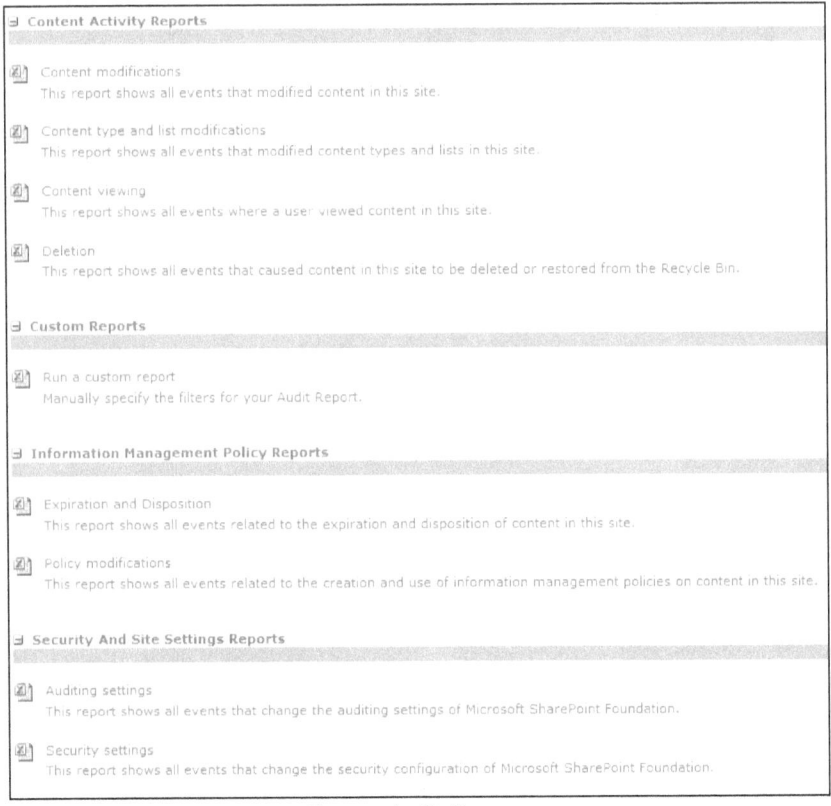

**Custom Audit Reports**

Custom Audit Log Reports may be configured to analyze user behavior transparently. These reports reveal what happened, when it happened, and who did it. It's as if 'Big Brother' is watching...

It's straight forward to set up a new report. You specify what Library to save the report in, set the date range, set which specific users to watch (if necessary), and select the type of events you wish to monitor. The one thing you really need to remember: you must *enable auditing* prior to using these types of reports. If auditing is not enabled, you will not have the information to report against. Custom Audit Log Reports are only available to authorized users.

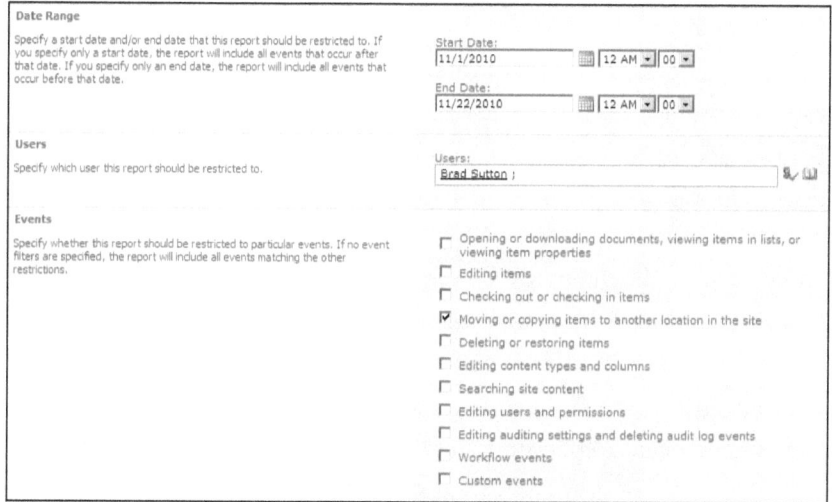

**Configure Custom Audit Report**

Your report will be generated and you can open it using Microsoft Excel. Use Excel to slice, dice, chart, and present these reports the way you want. This information helps with troubleshooting "mysterious" occurrences such as a user deleting a file and restoring it later. You will have a report showing who did what, and when they did it. This type of information is very helpful with keeping user confidence in the solution.

## Information Management Policies

SharePoint Information Management Policies are used to automate who has access to content, what they can do with it, and what the content retention rules are. Many orgs utilize Information

Management Policies to ensure compliance with regulations, standards, and even internal processes.

Orgs may have a need to keep copies of documents for seven years, or delete documents 24 months after creation. SharePoint may be used to set up, enforce, and monitor policies to track documents, control access to documents, and control how long to retain these documents.

Information Management Policies establish rules for the different types of content being used within your org. These rules are called Policy Features. You may create a Policy Template and associate it with an entire Site Collection, a specific Content Type, Document Library, or even a specific List. You have the flexibility to control different types of content and at what level you wish to enforce this control.

## Summary

Continuity may be sustained with proper organization and minimal disruption. Use the following concepts to ensure continuity and instill user confidence.

Don't settle for the default settings. **Configure Document Libraries** to optimize organization and maximize findability.

Configure the two-stage **Recycle Bin** to optimize the balance between Item restoration timeframes and available hard drive space.

Use Site **Usage Reports** to review general web analytics information, and Custom **Audit Reports** for precise usage monitoring.

Use **Information Management Policies** for automating organizational policies such as content retention and records management.

# Search

Your org is wasting a full month of *actual work time* every year due to findability issues. Imagine it takes a user five minutes to locate *something*. Maybe they need a Word document, a spreadsheet, a template, a donor record, or an email they know they've seen recently. Now imagine each user has to find *something* three times a day. They are spending five minutes each time when it should only take 30 seconds; that's 4.5 minutes wasted three times per day per user – 13.5 minutes each day! If this is happening to 10 users, then you are wasting over two hours *each day*. If your org averages 260 days per year, then you are wasting a lot of time!

Most people are presumably finding the information they need to perform their job. However, most people do not let anyone know how difficult it is to find information. Perhaps they just don't want to make a fuss, or maybe they just don't know any better. Regardless, it's taking them an exorbitant amount of time just to locate what they need to do their job. This has massive productivity ramifications.

| sharepoint for nonprofits | × | Search |
|---|---|---|

**Google Search Box**

Google spoiled us. We want to use a single search field and type in a word or two. We expect the technology to find exactly what we need and, of course, to find it quickly! This has changed everyone. Search is a major concern for everyone: staff, members, volunteers, donors, board members. In the past couple of years, even board members have been a catalyst for implementing a new technology at an org due to the fact that the search on the public-facing website was unusable. Users are accustomed to quickly finding exactly what they are looking for, yet they cannot find anything they're looking for on your website.

## SharePoint Search

SharePoint Search technology provides many components to deliver a rich search experience for your users. Here's how it works: The crawler/indexer crawls content and records its findings to an index file. The index file itself lives on the server hard drive. When someone issues a search, the search server retrieves results from the index file and displays them to the user. There are some fantastic books written on just the SharePoint Search engine.

SharePoint Search has enormous potential, but you should understand its many facets to support your org's objectives.

## Using Search

By default, the SharePoint Search box, where you enter a keyword or phrase and submit the search, is located in the upper right corner of the page. Search is supposed to be easy. Users expect instant and relevant results to be delivered using whatever magic necessary.

Depending on the Site Template being used, you may also see a dropdown for selecting the Search Scope.

**Search Box with Scope Dropdown**

The Search Scope dropdown allows the user to refine the search before they submit their query (more about Search Scopes later). The Search button is located to the right of the search box, the magnifying glass 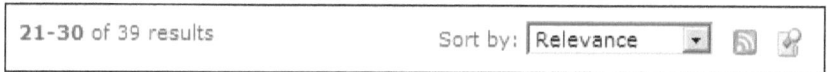 , and is used to submit your search.

To perform a search, simply enter the word or phrase you wish to search for in the search box and click the Search button. You're off to see the results.

## Search Results

SharePoint Search Results use Security Trimming so users will only see results which they have been granted permission to read. The Security enforced by SharePoint is carried through the Search Results.

Search results are displayed on the Search Results Page. This is a Page (the SharePoint kind) which has specific Web Parts for displaying the search results and other relevant search information.

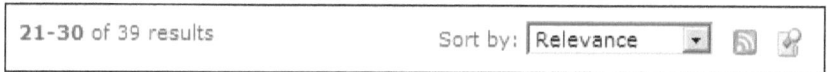

| 21-30 of 39 results | | Sort by: Relevance ▾ | 🔊 | 🔍 |

**Search Results have Result Count, Sort, RSS, and Find**

Results often span several pages, so SharePoint shows you how many results are being displayed on the page you are currently viewing. SharePoint also displays how many total results your search returned, and how long it took to process your search request.

Search results are displayed 10 at a time by default. Pagination controls are displayed at the top and bottom of the search result page. You can configure Search Web Parts to display more or less than 10 results at a time.

Depending on the version of SharePoint being used and which features are enabled, you will see a variation of Search Results.

**Result Thumbnail, Preview, and View in Browser**

There will be an icon, title, thumbnail (which is dependent upon the document type and features), a snippet of content, author information, date, size, URL, and a link to view in browser (also dependent upon the document type and features).

## Hit Highlighting

The Title is a hyperlink to the actual content (Page, document, file, image, Site, etc). Within the title and content preview, SharePoint highlights the word or phrase you searched for by making it bold. This is called "Hit Highlighting."

Below the title is the description. The description is a brief piece of text dynamically pulled from the actual content. SharePoint decides what to display here based on many factors.

The URL of the search result is located below the description. This lets you know the location of the actual Page, document, List Item, etc.

To the right of the URL is the file size. This is useful if you don't particularly feel like waiting for a huge document to load. The author and last date modified are displayed to the right of the file size. All of this information helps you decide if it's the search result you are looking for.

## Search Result Alerts

The Alert function allows you to sign up for an automated email notification. This notification is sent to your email address (or text-message to your phone) when the Search Results have changed in any way. For example, if a new document is uploaded to the Site and the document is relevant to your Search Result Alert, SharePoint will send you an email notification. When signing up for Search Result Alerts, you can title the alert and choose the types of changes you want to receive the alert for. Your options include:

New items in search results, Existing items have changed or All changes. Furthermore, you can choose how often you want to receive these alerts. Options include: **Send a daily summery** or **Send a weekly summery**. You can unsubscribe yourself from Search Result Alerts at any time. Alerts you subscribe to may be centrally managed by following the link "View my existing alerts on this site."

# RSS

RSS is a very popular way of syndicating or sharing content. RSS (Really Simple Syndication) is a widely adopted format compatible with many platforms and technologies. RSS is commonly used for news and blog websites, but can also be used for distributing other types of content, including pictures, audio or video.

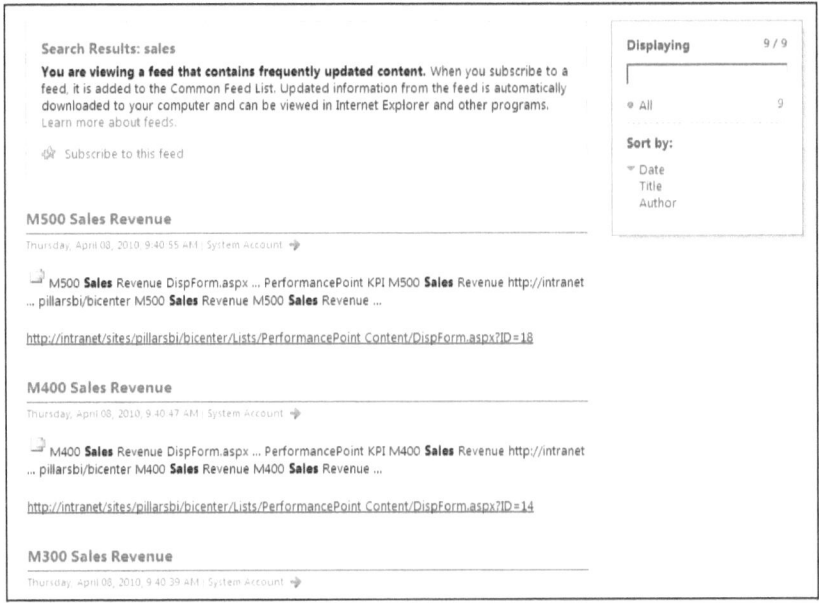

**Search Results RSS Feed**

When you click on the SharePoint Search Results RSS link, you are directed to the actual RSS feed for Search Results based upon your query.

## Search Refinements

Search Refinements are a welcome addition to the 2010 release of the SharePoint platform. Search Refinements are used to further filter search results based on metadata. After the search is performed, the metadata from the search result set is displayed in the Refinements panel. Only metadata with at least one corresponding search result will be displayed in the panel. This means you will never click on one of the Refinement links and receive a "no results found" message. By default, Refinements are displayed to the left of the search results and include the following:

> Result Type filters document type.
> Site filters Content Sources
> Author
> Modified Date
> Other tags or keywords contained in the search result set

You can configure other Search Refinements as necessary for your SharePoint Search implementation. You may choose to use metadata, including relevant items such as "Member Info", "Donor Info", "Volunteer Info" or even the Tags created and used by users.

Result Type
Any Result Type
Web Page (48)
Microsoft Word (16)
Microsoft Powe... (15)
Microsoft Excel (4)
show more ∨

Site
Any Site
intranet.conto... (94)

Author
Any Author
System Account (45)
Erika Cheley (34)
Tad Orman (13)
Sangya Singh (5)
show more ∨

Modified Date
Any Modified Date
Past Year (94)

Company
Any Company
Microsoft (12)
Bearings (1)
Contoso (1)
Eaton (1)
show more ∨

## Advanced Search

The Advanced Search page provides you with more precise searching capabilities. At its core, the Advanced Search Page is just a Page containing the Advanced Search Web Part. This search interface allows you to be very specific about what you are looking for.

➢ **All of these words** allow you to search for content containing ALL specified words, in any order. In traditional Boolean operations, this is similar to "AND."

➢ **The exact phrase** allows you to search for content containing words in the exact order you specify.

➢ **Any of these words** allows you to search for content containing any of the words you specify. In traditional Boolean operations, this is similar to "OR."

➢ **None of these words** allows you to search for content which does not contain specific words. In traditional Boolean operations, this is similar to "NOT."

The Advanced Search area also includes options for Language, Result Type, and Property Restrictions.

Find documents that have...

All of these words:
The exact phrase:
Any of these words:
None of these words:

Only the language(s): ☐ English
☐ French
☐ German
☐ Japanese
☐ Simplified Chinese
☐ Spanish
☐ Traditional Chinese

Result type: [All Results ▼]

**Add property restrictions...**

Where the Property... [(Pick Property) ▼] [Contains ▼] [_____] [And ▼] ✢

[Search]

**Advanced Search**

The Result Type, simply titled "Documents", is used for returning Page- or File-based results. In other words, selecting this option will prevent SharePoint List Items (like Calendar Events) from being returned in your search results. This option will still return PowerPoint Presentations and Excel files, as well as Microsoft Word Documents and even SharePoint Pages.

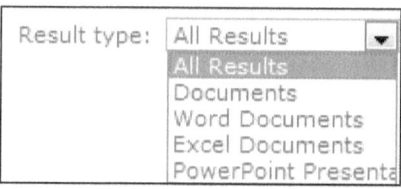

**Search by Result Type**

The "Add property restrictions..." area of Advanced Search allows you to build a search using specified properties (or metadata). For example, you could specify you only want results Last Modified in the previous Fiscal Year which were Authored by either Sean Bordner or John Stover.

| Add property restrictions... | | | | |
|---|---|---|---|---|
| Where the Property... | Last Modified Dat ▼ | Earlier than ▼ | 10/30/2010 | And ▼ |
| | Last Modified Dat ▼ | Later than ▼ | 10/30/2009 | And ▼ |
| | Author ▼ | Equals ▼ | John Stover | Or ▼ |
| | Author ▼ | Equals ▼ | Sean Bordner | And ▼ ✛ ═ |

Search

**Specify Search Properties**

The real power of the Advanced Search is the criteria described above is additive. You can specify any combination of keywords, languages, or restrictions. You can have zero, one or more restrictions apply to your search.

## Search Syntax

The maximum length of a query cannot exceed 1,024 characters. The easiest way to perform a search is to simply enter a word in the search box and click the search button. By default, SharePoint search is not case-sensitive, which means you can type in upper case, lower case, or a mix; and still get the same search results.

When more than one word is entered into the search box, SharePoint uses the AND query. The AND query ensures only results containing all the words entered are returned. This is not the same as entering a phrase into the search box.

Phrases are entered into the search box by enclosing the words in quotation marks. For example: "Employee Handbook" would be wrapped with quotes if you want SharePoint to treat it as a phrase. When SharePoint search treats a query as a phrase, it only returns results containing the exact match, in the exact order you specified.

You can also tell the search engine to exclude results with specific words in them by entering a minus sign (-) in front of the word or phrase you wish to exclude. For example: Employee –Handbook would return results relevant to the word "Employee", but not if the result also contained the word "Handbook" within its content.

Another powerful option is the use of properties or metadata. Property based queries simply follow the format of <property name>:<value>. For example, if you wanted to find all documents authored by Sean Bordner, you could make use of the Author Property on the Advanced Search Page. Or, you could just enter **Author:Sean Bordner** into the Search box.

You can even combine these capabilities into a single search. Let's say you knew the guy's name starts with 'S', and he authored an employee document, but it wasn't the Employee Handbook. You can't remember exactly what it was called, or where it was located, but you need to find it. No problem! You could jump back to the Advanced Search Page or you could simply enter Employee – Handbook Author: S and let the SharePoint search engine find it for you!

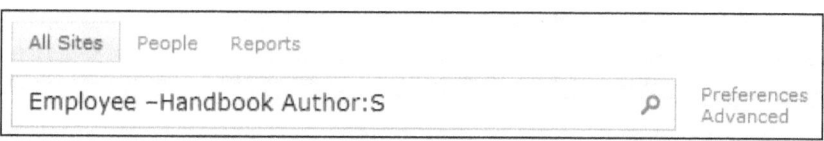

**Use Properties in the Search Box**

---

**Find documents that have...**

| | |
|---|---|
| All of these words: | Employee |
| The exact phrase: | |
| Any of these words: | |
| None of these words: | Handbook |
| Only the language(s): | ☐ English |
| | ☐ French |
| | ☐ German |
| | ☐ Japanese |
| | ☐ Simplified Chinese |
| | ☐ Spanish |
| | ☐ Traditional Chinese |
| Result type: | All Results ▼ |

**Add property restrictions...**

Where the Property... | Author ▼ | Contains ▼ | S | And ▼ ✛

Search

Use Properties on the Advanced Search Page

# Content Sources

A Content Source is a location which should be crawled by the Search Engine. Content Sources can extend beyond the boundaries of your SharePoint Sites. Content Sources can point to external websites, Exchange folders, network drives, and even external databases and line of business applications and systems (for example: AMS, CRM, Database, HR, Ecommerce, etc...). Configuring and managing Content Sources are not within the scope of this book, but can be achieved from the Central Administration Site in Search Application Services.

### Search Crawl Schedule

SharePoint allows you to schedule when it crawls each Content Source. It is important to consider a variety of things (like backups, patches, updates, heavy site usage, etc...) when planning your Crawl

---

Schedule to avoid conflicts and unnecessary overhead. Many factors come in to play when determining how your Crawl Schedule will impact the overall performance of your SharePoint solution. Detailed Crawl Schedule planning and management is out of the scope of this book. Your SharePoint Administrator will plan a Crawl Schedule that optimizes your infrastructure's capabilities.

## Search Scopes

Imagine your shiny, new SharePoint environment. You are using it to change the world. You have configured Search to use a variety of new Content Sources for your members and volunteers. You've also created Content Sources for your public-facing website, commerce site, event management site, four different government agency sites, 15 chapter sites, and a few affiliate organizations. You know you want your SharePoint search to be *the* portal for all users to find *any* information related to your org – whether you are the original content publisher or not.

All of this content is referred to as the *corpus*. The corpus is all of the indexed content, stored in such a way which SharePoint can quickly search. Now imagine you want to perform a search on a subset of your corpus. Enter Search Scopes.

A Search Scope is a subdivision of your entire corpus used for specific search purposes. You could have a Search Scope just for products (like a bookstore search). You could have a Search Scope for affiliates, government information, website content only, or member content only. The capabilities are limitless. You can use Search Scopes to build dedicated Search tools – like a Member

Directory or Job Board – but SharePoint can use the Search Scopes for filtering as well.

The search box can optionally display a Search Scope dropdown allowing the user to pre-filter their desired search (examples: People, Only Search This Site, All Sites, etc...). Furthermore, you can add Search Scopes as tabs on the Search Results Page.

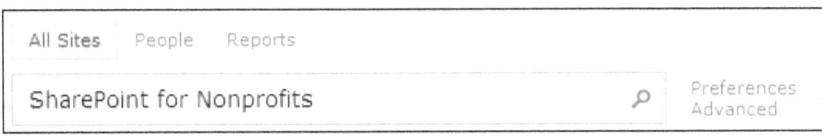

**Display Search Scopes as Tabs**

## Authoritative Pages

Search authoritative pages are essential for promoting specific pages of your Site or other websites within the organic search results section of the Search Results Page. Pages may also be demoted if you do not want certain Pages to be ranked as well.

## Search Best Bets and Keywords

Best Bets are similar to Sponsored Links seen on popular Internet search engines today. Best Bets target specific pieces of content to users searching for a specific keyword or phrase. For example, if you had an upcoming event called "Child Education Conference", you could ensure its information Page is returned in search results when users search using the keyword "children" and "kid" and "conference." You may have multiple Best Bets running simultaneously. Best Bets are commonly used for promoting events and otherwise important content. The Search Usage Reports (discussed later in this chapter) can help you understand what users are looking for and NOT finding – a perfect example of when to use a Best Bets.

By default, Best Bets are represented with a star icon. The Best Bets Web Part is used to display them. As with all SharePoint Web Parts, you can move them around the page, and add or delete them from a page.

☆ **Event**
Don't forget to register for our Annual Conference.

☆ ORG Annual Conference
http://intranet.contoso.com/wiki

▦ Gears Project Home
... files or on the calendar to create new team **events**. Use the links in the getting started section ...
files or on the calendar to create new team **events**. Use the links in the getting started section ...
Authors: Contoso Administrator System Account   Date: 5/6/2010   Size: 118KB
http://intranet.contoso.com

**SharePoint Search Best Bets**

The first step in setting up Best Bets is determining the URL of the page you want users directed to. This can be any URL, internal or external website, SharePoint or not. You should also have at least one Keyword in mind (more than one is even better). Additionally, you should have the text already prepared which will make up the best bet; this includes the Title and Description. In other words; when someone types a Keyword into the Search Box and clicks the search button, you want them to see [Title and Description]. When they click on it, you want this [URL] to load.

If you want even more capability and search power, look into FAST Search for SharePoint. FAST adds User Context capabilities to model search behavior differently for various user collections as well as Visual Best Bets and Site Promotion/Demotion in the context of users. FAST is incredible.

## Customizing the Search Results Page

You can customize the search results page to compliment your business objectives. Of course, you'll want to brand the Search Results page to match your website with colors, styles, fonts, etc. The Master Page applied to the Site will handle the branding of these elements. Branding the search results page to match your Site is just part of the equation. You can configure the Search Results Page to format and display results, Best Bests, and related content in a way which will compliment your business objectives.

The SharePoint Search results page consists of several Web Parts. Each Web Part performs a specific task. You may configure each Web Part to behave as desired. You can arrange the placement of these Web Parts as you wish. You can remove Web Parts you don't want to use, and add multiple instances of the same Web Part as needed.

## Search Center Site Template

The Search Center Template is a SharePoint Site Template used specifically for creating Search Centers. Your SharePoint Site may have zero, one, or multiple Search Centers, depending on your specific requirements and business objectives. Search Centers can be thought of as a search "hub", and are typically used as a central search area of a Site. They provide all the necessary components for users to quickly and easily find what they are looking for. While it is common to provide a search box on every page of your site, once a search is issued, the resulting search results page is typically located within the Search Center itself.

Once your Search Center is created, you can add tabs to further enhance the search experience. Tabs are typically used to provide users the ability to search specific Scopes. For example, you may only want to search your organization's internal intranet Site, or maybe you only want to search your organization's extranet Site or public-facing website. Perhaps you want to search for people or receive results only from external Sites. For more information about Search Scopes, see the "Search Scopes" section of this chapter.

## Search Tabs

A search tab is just a link to a Search Result Page which has been set up to display a specific result type. For example, the "People" tab is used if you are looking for a specific person. The "All Sites" tab is used for searching everywhere – the entire corpus. If your search has been set up to crawl external sites, a tab called "External Sites" might be useful.

**Search Tabs**

Since a tab is really just a link to a Page, the first step involved in adding a new tab is to create a new Page. Once you have created your new search results Page, it's simply a matter of adding the new tab to point to it, and configuring the new Page to honor the appropriate Search Scope.

## Federated Search

The SharePoint search engine also provides federated search capabilities. Federated search enables the search to be processed by another search engine, not the SharePoint search engine. The search term is passed to the external search engine (like Bing for example). Bing performs the search and returns results to be displayed on your search result page. Results are displayed within the Federated Search Web Part, typically located alongside the results returned from your SharePoint search engine.

| Available Connectors | | | |
|---|---|---|---|
| **News** | **Media** | **Blogs** | **Information Resources** |
| Bing News | Bing Image | Google Blog Search | Bing |
| Business Week | Flickr | | Bing Local |
| Google News | Yahoo! Images | | Encyclopedia Britannica |
| The Register | YouTube | | MSDN |
| Yahoo! News | | | TechNet |
| | | | Wikipedia |
| | | | Yahoo! |

**SharePoint Federated Search**

Microsoft provides an online gallery of preconfigured Federated Search connections, making this configuration as simple as a click of the mouse. However, you're not limited to only those preconfigured connections provided by Microsoft, as you can integrate your Federated Search with any other available search technology.

## Search Web Parts

SharePoint provides search specific Web Parts. Understanding these Web Parts will allow you to provide highly relevant content to your users, as well as deliver rich information on Pages which aren't even used for searching purposes.

| Web Parts | | |
|---|---|---|
| Advanced Search Box | Search Action Links | Top Federated Results |
| Dual Chinese Search | Search Best Bets | |
| Federated Results | Search Box | |
| People Refinement Panel | Search Core Results | |
| People Search Box | Search Paging | |
| People Search Core Results | Search Statistics | |
| Refinement Panel | Search Summary | |
| Related Queries | Search Visual Best Bet | |

**Search Web Parts**

We're not going to cover a full list of all search related Web Parts in detail, but it is worth noting a few.

## Advanced Search Box

This Web Part is used on the Advanced Search Page by default. It provides a way to perform very specific searches based on more than just a keyword or phrase. This is a powerful Web Part. The functionality of this Web Part is covered in the "Advanced Search" section of this chapter.

## Search Best Bets

The Best Bets functionality was discussed earlier. This Web Part allows you to provide the Best Bets functionality anywhere within your Sites.

## Search Core Results

The Search Core Results Web Part is used for displaying the actual search results, and is located on Search Results Pages by default. This Web Part can be used for more than just displaying results to users who typed in a word and clicked search.

The Search Core Results Web Part may be used to display the results of a pre-defined search term. You can use this Web Part wherever you want. It is not just for the Search Results Pages. Perhaps you have an article involving health issues, and to the right of this article you want to display the most current related information available. You can display the five most recent Pages containing the word "health." This can be accomplished using the Search Core Results Web Part by simply setting the Fixed Query property to "health." This Web Part also allows you to set the Results Per Page to five, as well as display results by Relevance using the Default Results View property.

The Web Part utilizes the Search Index, which means the results will be the five most relevant documents, List Items, articles, products, or events for the word "health." Also, the list of relevant content is automatically updated as the SharePoint Search algorithm identifies newer or more relevant content involving "health." This Web Part provides the same capabilities discussed earlier about Search Results such as Alerts, RSS, and the ability to control how many lines of descriptive text are displayed along with the results.

## Search Usage Reports

Web Analytics such as Site visits and browsing paths are helpful to have, but are marginally useful on websites where users are searching for information. Search Analytics provides the key to determining what your members, donors, and volunteers are actively seeking. Understanding how users are utilizing your search engine allows you to continuously make the Site better for them.

It's important to understand what users are looking for and what they are finding and clicking on. It's perhaps even more important to understand what they are searching for and NOT finding.

This information is all tracked in SharePoint. SharePoint offers two levels of search reporting; SharePoint Administrator level reports and Site Collection Administrator level reports. SharePoint Administrator level reports are only available from the Central Administration Site. However, if you belong to the Site Collection Administrator group, you can access the second level of search reports from your Site.

## Summary Report

This report shows the available Search Analytics for the date range specified, as well as the change trend from the preceding date range.

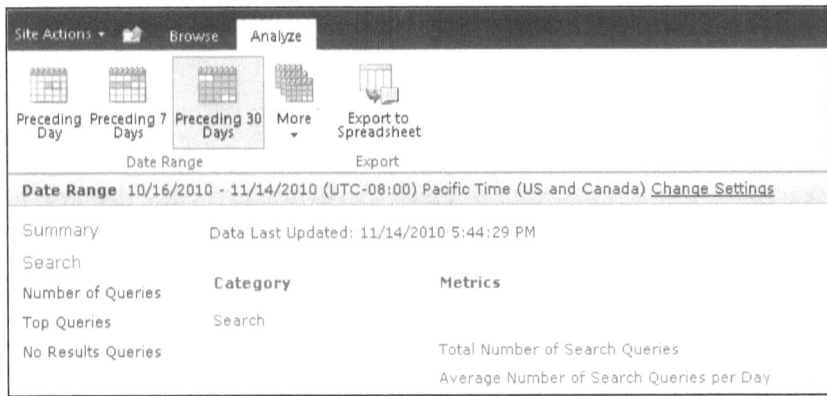

**SharePoint Search Analytics**

## Number of Queries

This report shows the number of search queries performed for the specified date range. Use this report to identify search query volume trends, and to determine times of high and low search activity.

**Number of Queries Report**

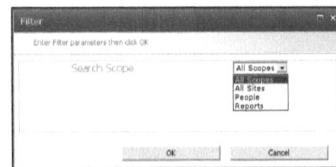

**Filter Report by Search Scope**

## Top Queries

This report shows the most popular search queries performed for the specified date range. Use this report to understand what types of information visitors are seeking.

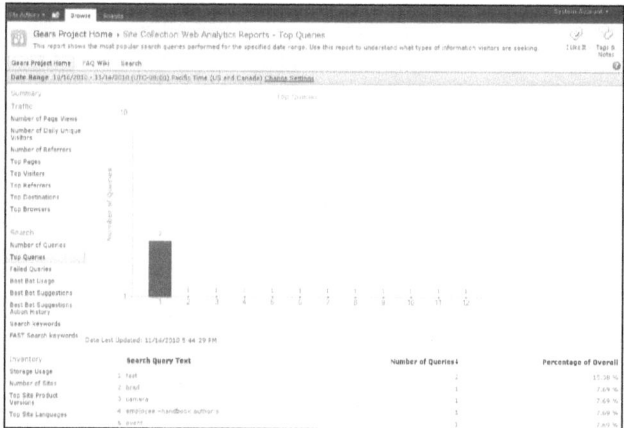

**Top Queries Report**

## Failed Queries

This report shows search queries which returned no search results. Use this report to identify search queries which might create user dissatisfaction, and to improve the findability of content.

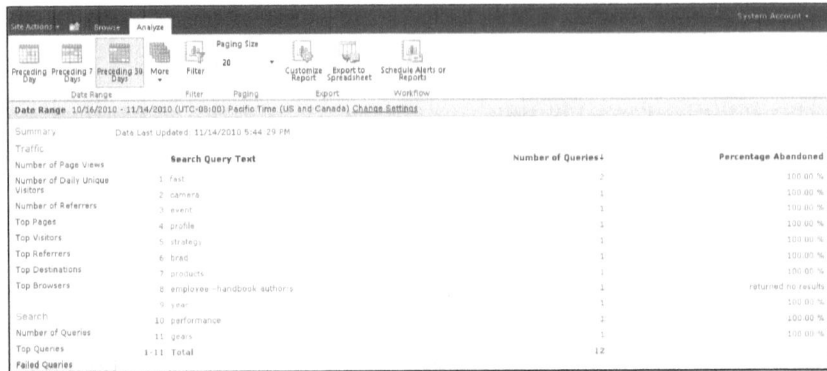

**Failed Queries Report**

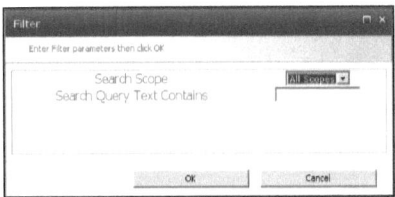

**Filter Report**

## Best Bet Usage

This report shows the number of click-throughs the Best Bets URLs received for search keywords. These Best Bets were either added manually on the Manage Keywords Page or added in response to the system recommendations in the Best Bet Suggestions report. Use this report to track the success of Best Bets.

## Best Bet Suggestions

This actionable report shows system suggestions for Best Bet URLs for certain search keywords. You may take action in the report by accepting or rejecting suggestions.

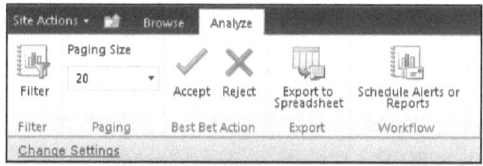

**Analyze Best Bets**

## Best Bet Suggestions Action History

This report shows the actions (accept or reject) which have been taken against the Best Bet Suggestions report.

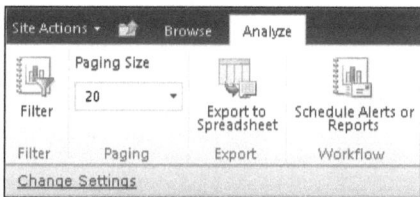

**Best Bet Action History**

# Summary

For many orgs, SharePoint Search is reason enough to install and configure SharePoint. Capable of indexing all of your org's content (within SharePoint or not), these tools are available to ensure users can find what they need, when they need it.

**Index content** in websites, SharePoint Sites, databases, AMS, CRM, member records, products, events, jobs, abstracts, magazines, and publications.

Index many **types of files** including PDF files, Office files (Word, Excel, PowerPoint, etc.), text files, and more.

Configure the **Search experience** for the right audience. Staff may need a different search experience than volunteers, but all audiences need a powerful search tool.

**Search Analytics** provide the insight to ensure you have the correct tools in place. Even more important, analytics provide the knowledge that you have the right *content* available, and that your users can easily find it!

# SharePoint Security

Perhaps not the sexiest topic, security is certainly among the most important. The SharePoint security model allows your org to lock down some of your content to only members while keeping some of your content open to the public. That's an example of a public-facing website with login access to the protected content.

The SharePoint security model allows your org to re-use your existing roles already populated in your AMS or CRM solution. You likely already have roles defined as committees, groups, chapters, councils, special interest groups, communities of practice, or any other logical grouping of users.

SharePoint can honor those roles and provide access to specific locations of your Site with varying levels of permissions based on the location and role combination. You can also leverage your existing Active Directory Security Groups.

To successfully accomplish any of this, you need an understanding of the SharePoint security model and how to tailor it to suit your org's specific needs. Understanding best practices related to SharePoint security will save you a lot of overhead with respect to ongoing security management.

Jumping around this chapter may result in confusion, so please read this chapter in proper sequence. We promise to keep it as concise as possible.

## SharePoint Site Groups

A SharePoint Site Group is just a group of users. You add users to each SharePoint Site Group. SharePoint Site Groups can be thought of as Roles with varying levels of permissions to various locations of your Site.

For example, you may have a SharePoint Site Group called "HR Staff" which has Read permission in most sections of your intranet. However, in the HR Site, your "HR Staff" SharePoint Site Group has been granted Read, Add, and Delete permissions.

This same principle applies throughout SharePoint and across the different permutations of the platforms' uses – whether you are using SharePoint for an intranet, extranet, member community, public-facing website, or all of these permutations.

You can create your own SharePoint Site Groups. Let's first look at the default SharePoint Site Groups available with any new Site.

- ➢ Visitors - Use this group to grant read permissions.

- ➢ Members - Use this group to grant contribute permissions.

- ➢ Approvers - Members of this group can edit and approve Pages, List Items, and documents.

- ➢ Owners - Use this group to grant full control permissions.

- ➢ Designers - Members of this group can edit Lists, Document Libraries, and Pages in the Site. Designers can create Master Pages and Page Layouts in the Master Page Gallery, and can change the behavior and appearance of each Site in the Site collection by using master Pages and CSS files.

➤ Hierarchy Managers - Members of this group can create Sites, Lists, List Items, and documents.

➤ Restricted Readers - Members of this group can view Pages and documents but cannot view historical versions or review user rights information.

➤ Style Resource Readers - Members of this group are given read permission to the Master Page Gallery and the Restricted Read permission to the Style Library. By default, all authenticated users are a member of this group. To further secure this Site, you can remove all authenticated users from or add users to this group.

Active Directory (AD) will almost certainly be used to store some of your users who access your SharePoint solution. In fact, most orgs end up looking something like this:

➤ Intranet Solution = User accounts in AD.

➤ Extranet Solution = Staff user accounts in AD while non-staff user accounts in AMS/CRM system.

➤ Public-facing Website Solution = Staff user accounts in AD and non-staff user accounts in AMS/CRM system. Users without user accounts can simply register to create an account in your AMS/CRM system.

Therefore, SharePoint's built-in ability to honor your existing Active Directory (AD) Security Groups not only saves time but also prevents you from having to manage individual user account permissions in multiple places. For example, you can simply define in SharePoint the existing AD Security Group (like Domain Users) which has Add, Modify, and Delete permissions in a particular Site.

You will undoubtedly have the need to create your own SharePoint Site Groups. A SharePoint Site Group can be thought of as a Role, and your org will need specific Roles (SharePoint Site Groups) different from those created by default during installation.

A key benefit of SharePoint Site Groups is that it's easier and faster to manage permissions at a Group level rather than at the individual user or Item level. Think in terms of "groups of users" who need the same permissions in a given location (Site, Subsite, Document Library or List).

When "Bob the Accountant" leaves your organization to spend time practicing Yoga in the Himalayas, how much work do you want to do ensuring his replacement has all the same permissions that Bob had throughout the Site? It would be nice to simply add the new person's account to the correct AD Security group(s) or make sure the new guy's account belongs to the same SharePoint Site Groups.

If you chose to ignore SharePoint Site Groups and configure permissions for individual accounts, you will need to figure out every single location where you granted rights to "Bob the Accountant." You will need to determine what permissions were granted at that location, remove Bob's account, and add the new person's account with the same permissions.

This is not even a realistic option. Without a third-party utility or writing scripts, you would need to manually check every single Site, Subsite, Library, List and Item. It's just not going to happen. Plan out your SharePoint Site Groups and stick to your plan when adding new users to your Site.

Here are the fields you fill out when creating a new SharePoint Site Group:

> **Name and About Me Description** - Type a descriptive name for your Site Group and add a description for the group. Do not skip the description even though it's not required. Take the extra 30 seconds and fill it out accurately. You will thank yourself 12 month later when you try to figure out why that Site Group was created.

> **Owner** - The owner can change anything about the group, such as adding and removing members, or deleting the group. Only one user or group can be the owner.

> **Group Settings** - Specify who has permission to see the list of group members, and who has permission to add and remove members from the group.

➤ **Membership Requests** - Specify whether to allow users to request membership in this group and allow users to request to leave the group. All requests will be sent to the e-mail address specified. If auto-accept is enabled, users will automatically be added or removed when they make a request. Caution: If you select 'yes' for the Auto-accept requests option, any user requesting access to this group will automatically be added as a member of the group and receive the permission levels associated with the group.

➤ **Give Group Permission to this Site** - Specify the permission level that you want members of this SharePoint group to have on this Site. If you do not want to give group members access to this Site, ensure that all checkboxes are unselected.

   o **Full Control** - Has full control.

   o **Design** - Can view, add, update, delete, approve, and customize.

   o **Contribute** - Can view, add, update, and delete List Items and documents.

   o **Read** - Can view Pages and List Items, and download documents.

   o **Approve** - Can edit and approve pages, List Items, and documents.

o   **Manage Hierarchy** - Can create Sites and edit Pages, List Items, and documents.

o   **Restricted Read** - Can view Pages and documents, but cannot view historical versions or user permissions.

o   **Records Center Web Service Submitters** – Can submit content to this Site using Web Services.

# SharePoint Permissions

SharePoint permissions can be divided into three main categories: *List Permissions, Site Permissions* and *Personal Permissions*.

The separation of permission categories is for organization purposes only. You can certainly mix any two or more permissions as needed.

## Site Permissions

➤   **Manage Permissions** - Create and change permission levels on the Web Site and assign permissions to users and groups.

➤   **View Web Analytics Data** - View reports on Web Site usage.

➤   **Create Subsites** - Create Subsites such as team Sites, Meeting Workspace Sites, and Document Workspaces.

➤ **Manage Web Site** - Grant the ability to perform all administration tasks for the Web Site, as well as manage content.

➤ **Add and Customize Pages** - Add, change, or delete HTML Pages or Web Part Pages, and edit the Web Site using a Microsoft SharePoint Foundation-compatible editor.

➤ **Apply Themes and Borders** - Apply a theme or borders to the entire Web Site.

➤ **Apply Style Sheets** - Apply a style sheet (.CSS file) to the Web Site.

➤ **Create Groups** - Create a group of users that can be used anywhere within the Site collection.

➤ **Browse Directories** - Enumerate files and folders in a Web Site using SharePoint Designer and Web DAV interfaces.

➤ **Use Self-Service Site Creation** - Create a Web Site using Self-Service Site Creation.

➤ **View Pages** - View pages in a Web Site.

➤ **Enumerate Permissions** - Enumerate permissions on the Web Site, List, folder, document, or List Item.

> **Browse User Information** - View information about users of the Web Site.

> **Manage Alerts** - Manage alerts for all users of the Web Site.

> **Use Remote Interfaces** - Use SOAP, Web DAV, the Client Object Model or SharePoint Designer interfaces to access the Web Site.

> **Use Client Integration Features** - Use features which launch client applications. Without this permission, users will have to work on documents locally and upload their changes.

> **Open** - Allows users to open a Web Site, List, or folder in order to access items inside that container.

> **Edit Personal User Information** - Allows a user to change his or her own user information, such as adding a picture.

| | | |
|---|---|---|
| ☐ | Team Site Members | SharePoint Contribute Group |
| ☐ | Team Site Owners | SharePoint Full Control Group |
| ☐ | Team Site Visitors | SharePoint Read Group |

**Site Permissions**

## List Permissions

> ➤ **Manage Lists** - Create and delete Lists, add or remove columns in a List, and add or remove public views of a List.

> ➤ **Override Check Out** - Discard or check in a document which is checked out to another user.

> ➤ **Add Items** - Add items to Lists, and add documents to document Libraries.

> ➤ **Edit Items** - Edit items in Lists, edit documents in document Libraries, and customize Web Part Pages in document Libraries.

> ➤ **Delete Items** - Delete items from a List, and documents from a document library.

> ➤ **View Items** - View items in Lists and documents in document Libraries.

> ➤ **Approve Items** - Approve a minor version of a List Item or document.

> ➤ **Open Items** - View the source of documents with server-side file handlers.

➢ **View Versions** - View past versions of a List Item or document.

➢ **Delete Versions** - Delete past versions of a List Item or document.

➢ **Create Alerts** - Create alerts.

➢ **View Application Pages** - View forms, views, and application pages. Enumerate Lists.

```
Permissions and Management

Delete this list

Save list as template

Permissions for this list

Workflow Settings

Generate file plan report

Enterprise Metadata and Keywords
Settings

Information management policy settings
```

**Mange List Permissions**

## Personal Permissions

➢ **Manage Personal Views** - Create, change, and delete personal views of Lists.

➢ **Add/Remove Personal Web Parts** - Add or remove personal Web Parts on a Web Part Page.

> ➤ **Update Personal Web Parts** - Update Web Parts to display personalized information.

## SharePoint Permission Levels

You've guessed it right; SharePoint Permission Levels are logical collections of permissions! Therefore, you could create a new Permission Level called "Chapter Leaders" and add the appropriate permissions to your new Permission Level.

**Name and Description**

Type a name and description for your permission level. The name is shown on the permissions page. The name and description are shown on the add users page.

Name:
Custom Permission for Chapter Leader

Description:
This custom permission is needed for Chapter Leaders.

**Permissions**

Choose which permissions to include in this permission level. Use the **Select All** check box to select or clear all permissions.

Select the permissions to include in this permission level.

☐ **Select All**

**List Permissions**

☐ Manage Lists - Create and delete lists, add or remove columns in a list, and add or remove public views of a list.

☐ Override Check Out - Discard or check in a document which is checked out to another user.

☐ Add Items - Add items to lists and add documents to document libraries.

☐ Edit Items - Edit items in lists, edit documents in document libraries, and customize Web Part Pages in document libraries.

☐ Delete Items - Delete items from a list and documents from a document library.

SharePoint Permission Levels

## Sites, Lists, and Item Level Permissions

Here's how it all comes together. SharePoint Site Groups are collections of users. Permission Levels are associated with Site

Groups relative to specific locations. Permission Levels are just a collection of permissions.

The only part we've not covered very well so far is the "locations" part we've mentioned a few times now. When we use the term "locations", we are referring to SharePoint objects. Specifically, we are referring to Sites, Subsites, Lists and Items. When you can answer the following question, you have a solid understanding of your SharePoint Security model:

**Q: Who can do what and where?**

**A Sample answer:** HR Members (SharePoint Site Group) have Contribute permissions (Permission Level) on the HR Subsite (location) and Restricted Read permissions (Permission Level) on the rest of the Site (location).

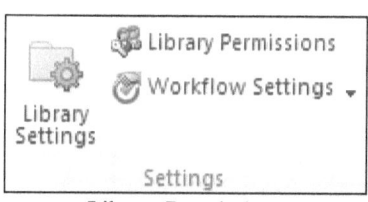

**Library Permissions**

SharePoint allows permissions to be assigned all the way down to the Item level. Remember an Item can be anything in a List, and practically *everything* in SharePoint is in a List.

Examples of Items in a List include: files in a Document Library, Events in a Calendar, names in a Contacts List, and entries in an Announcements List, just to name a few.

You can select a specific file in a Document Library and assign permissions to it which are different from all the other files in the Document Library if you needed to. While SharePoint allows this, you should not make this a common practice because you would be creating a security *management* nightmare.

**Item-level security should be the exception and not the rule.**

It is far better to control permissions at the highest level possible (Site or Subsite) and not the lowest (Item). Ask yourself if you can set permissions at the Site level which work without exceptions. If not, what exceptions are there? Perhaps the exceptions only occur on a Document Library. Set the Document Library to stop inheriting permissions from the Site, and use unique permissions. It's still better to manage permissions at the List level than at the Item level. A Document Library is at the List level (it's a list of files).

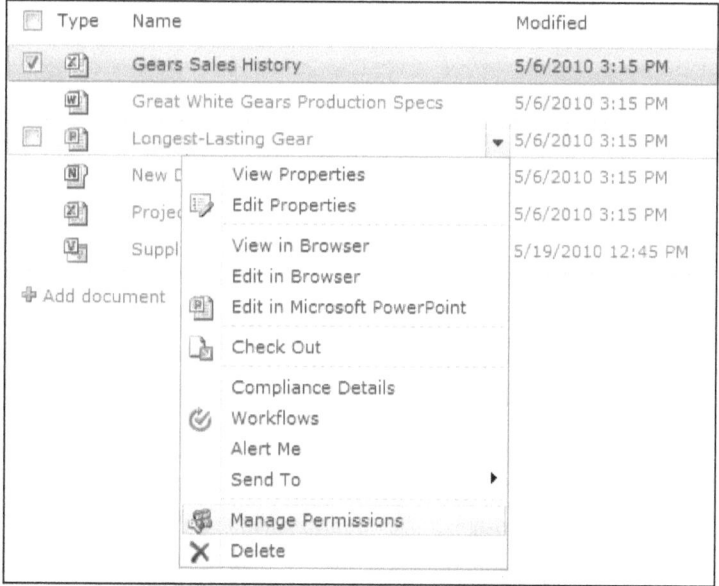

**Mange SharePoint Item Level Permissions**

# Inheritance

Items inherit permissions from the List which contain them. The List inherits permissions from the Subsite which contains it. The Subsite inherits permissions from the parent Subsite which contains it. And it goes until you reach the top level Site. It is that simple! You can break this inheritance at any point in the chain as needed. You can just as easily re-inherit permissions as needed.

As a matter of best practices, you should manage permissions at the highest level possible. You will sometimes need to break this rule and add specific permissions at the Item level, but be sure to make this the exception rather than the rule.

## Security Trimming

Security trimming refers to SharePoint's ability to dynamically remove Items from the display which the user does not have permission to see. Security trimming occurs in several places:

> **Navigation** – SharePoint will not display navigation Items when the user doesn't have READ permissions at the very least. SharePoint will only display navigation Items to a user having READ or greater permissions.

> **Search Results** – SharePoint will not display search results to a user without READ permissions at the very least. SharePoint will only display search results to a user having READ or greater permissions on the Items.

> **List Views** – SharePoint will not display Items in a List to a user without READ permissions at the very least. SharePoint will only display List items to a user having READ or greater permissions.

> **Web Parts** – SharePoint will not display Items in aggregating Web Parts such as the Content Query Web Part to any user without READ permissions at the very least. SharePoint will only display List items to a user having READ or greater permissions.

## Site Collection Administrator

The Super-User account of the SharePoint world is the Site Collection Administrator. Technically, the Site Collection

Administrator is a special SharePoint group which typically has two users: one is the primary and the other is the backup.

The Site Collection Administrator group can be designated from the Site Settings Page in the SharePoint Site, but you must already be a Site Collection Administrator in order to do so.

Site Collection Administrators can read, add, delete, or modify everything in all Sites contained within the Site Collection. Site Collection Administrators can also add and remove users from the various Sites contained within the Site Collection.

However, Site Collection Administrators may be restricted should the need arise. For example, perhaps the IT Pro shouldn't actually have permissions to see confidential HR files. Restricting this access is handled from the Central Administration Site by configuring the appropriate Web Application Policy.

## Security Administration

While Site Collection Administrators can be assigned both from the Central Administration Site and from the actual Site Collection itself, it's usually easier to manage security at the Site Collection level.

From the Site Collection Site Settings web interface, you can manage all security settings for the Site, including who belongs to the Site Collection Administrators group.

**Security Administration**

From the Site Settings page, you can access the users, permissions, and groups sections, as well as the Site Collection Administrations. The Site Collections Administrators Link is only visible to Site Collection Administrators. If you are not a Site Collection Administrator, you will not see the link, nor will you see any of the Site Collection administration settings. Security trimming at work!

It's fairly straight forward to create new SharePoint Site Groups and add users to the groups. It should literally take you no longer than a few minutes from the Site Settings Page to create a new "Committee" Site Group and populate it with the appropriate user accounts.

Creating permission levels and assigning specific permissions to these levels is also straight forward. If you are spending a lot of time or effort managing SharePoint security, there are some great third-party utilities available which can enhance your security administration experience.

## Summary

The SharePoint security model provides the flexibility to honor your existing AMS or CRM based roles, in addition to your existing Active Directory Security Groups. Understanding how SharePoint security components are used according to best practices will ensure your solution is highly secure and manageable.

**SharePoint Site Groups** can be thought of as roles. Site Groups can be easily created and have appropriate permissions in various locations throughout your Site. Users may belong to multiple Site Groups as needed.

There are three main categories of **permissions**: Site permissions, List permissions and Personal permissions. Permissions represent specific actions such as Read, Add, Update, or Delete.

**Permission Levels** are a set of specific permissions. Permission Levels may be easily created, and SharePoint provides many default Permission Levels to get you started. Permission Levels may be associated with specific Site Groups (roles) to control what those users are permitted to see and do.

**Security Trimming** is prevalent throughout the SharePoint experience. Security Trimming is the act of NOT displaying things to users who do not have "Read" permissions at the very least. This automatically happens within the navigation of your Site and within the search results.

The **Site Collection Administrator** has "super user" access across the entire Site Collection. Access can however be restricted at the Web Application level should the need arise.

Most security settings can be configured at the Site Collection level with **Security Administration** making it straight forward to manage. Third-party utilities further reduce the effort involved with ongoing security administration.

# Maintain a Healthy Environment

Sustaining a healthy SharePoint environment requires a Maintenance Plan. The Maintenance Plan should be devised using a core set of maintenance planning best practices.

It is important to keep an open line of communication between your users and the IT folks responsible for the maintenance of your SharePoint solution. One great way to do this is by performing periodic surveys among your users in order to determine what they need from your Site. We recommend conducting such surveys no more than once a year and at most twice.

It makes sense to use the native SharePoint Survey template for this effort. Use SharePoint logs and reports to determine which sections of your Site are being used, and merge this data with your survey results to help identify what can be improved.

Part of your Maintenance Plan should include archiving obsolete content and Sites. Make sure your users understand this is happening and are educated on how to locate archived information. Execute your archival actions at a predictable frequency. Users should have a clear understanding of the archival schedule.

Review Site Permissions regularly. This exercise may be used to remove Permissions for users who have left the org or simply changed groups or projects.

Plan *and test* backups of your Site content on a regular schedule. Document the frequency of backups as well as the processes followed in restoring content when needed. This planning will vary based on factors such as the amount of content to backup, full versus incremental backups, performance factors, and your solution's availability requirements.

Everyone says this yet very few do it: ***test your restore process***.

## Site Collections

A SharePoint Site Collection is a group of Sites which can be managed together. Sites within a Site Collection may have shared components such as security, features, look and feel, and navigation. A Site Collection has one "top-level Site" with any number of Subsites below it.

A Subsite refers to any Site within a Site Collection that is not the top-level Site itself. A Subsite may inherit navigation and/or permissions from its parent, or these permissions can be specified and managed separately.

Site Collection users may create Subsites if they have proper permissions, but Site Collections themselves must be created by someone with Site Collection Administration permissions.

Sometimes it's better to create an entirely new Site Collection, while other times it makes more sense just to create a Subsite below an existing Site Collection. For instance, if you have many sub-committees which fit within a larger committee, it makes sense to use Subsites to manage each sub-committee.

Part of your Maintenance Plan should address adjusting Site Collection Quotas if needed. Site Collection quotas are managed in the Central Administration Site. Quotas are used to control how large a specific Site Collection may become.

If a Site Collection is growing near the quota size limit, you can either adjust the Quota to a larger size or reduce the overall size of the Site Collection. Keep in mind that these Quotas are in place for a reason. It is better to first attempt to reduce the overall size of the Site Collection.

Monitoring and removing unused Site Collections should also be a part of your Maintenance Plan. This process may be automated, and the automation steps depend on your version of SharePoint.

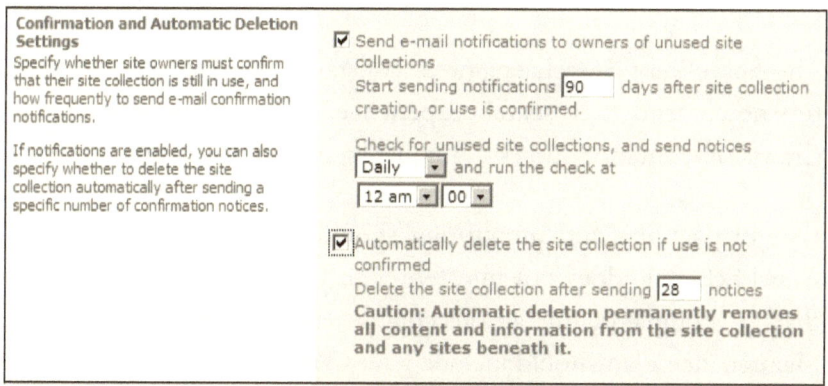

**Automate Content Retention**

Your Plan needs to identify the rules to determine if a Site Collection is unused, as well as the actions being taken in such cases.

## Taxonomy Evolution

The way you classify information will change over time. Therefore you need a plan for updating your taxonomy. Conduct a high level content classification session annually with the appropriate individuals (department heads, chapter leaders, committee Site users, etc...) to determine any tags which need to be added or to identify any restructuring which should occur.

Ensure your Maintenance Plan includes a scheduled window for updating your taxonomy. Most orgs should plan on reviewing and updating their taxonomy on an annual basis, but you may choose to do so more frequently depending on specific org requirements.

## Search Tuning

The SharePoint Search engine is constantly working to provide a top notch, end user search experience. This includes scheduled Crawls of Content Sources – not just your SharePoint Site.

Careful planning and monitoring should take place to ensure the Crawl Schedule does not interfere with your backup schedule, and that it completes in an acceptable amount of time. Your Maintenance Plan should include your Crawl Schedule for both Full Crawls and Incremental Crawls.

| Type | ⦿ Daily | | |
|---|---|---|---|
| Select the type of schedule. | ○ Weekly | | |
| | ○ Monthly | | |
| **Settings** | Run every: * | 1 | days |
| Type the schedule settings. | Starting time: | 12:00 AM ▾ | |
| | ☐ Repeat within the day | | |
| | Every: | 5 | minutes |
| | For: | 1440 | minutes |

**SharePoint Search Crawl Schedule**

Additionally, you will periodically need to create new Content Sources to crawl, as well as remove Content Sources which are no longer being utilized. This maintenance should also be planned and scheduled as part of your Maintenance Plan.

## User Interface Evolution

Keep the overarching user interface (UI) up to date. The UI is the look and feel of your Site, and it should reinforce your Information Architecture (IA) which is the structure and taxonomy of your Site.

You probably do not want to drastically change the look and feel of your Site on a regular basis, but you do want to keep it current and fresh. For example, ensuring the most recent logo version is used throughout the Site. Your org Branding Guidelines should also be carefully observed and adhered to. A consistent message is the best way to avoid confusion and frustration, and to maximize user adoption with members, volunteers, and especially staff.

Determine the appropriate time of year to re-visit your Site UI and make the required updates. In most cases, this should be executed no more than once a year. If the changes being made to your Site are drastic, make sure you inform your users well in advance of the update. Let them know what's about to change, and get them excited about it by pointing out the benefits.

## Change Management

Your Maintenance Plan should include a change management section. This section needs to outline the process used to ensure data continuity. For example, during the migration process it is not uncommon to keep the existing, OLD website running as usual while you migrate content to the NEW Site. During this time, any new content added to the OLD website should be accounted for and also migrated to the NEW Site.

Many orgs handle the change management issue by simply placing the OLD website in read-only mode at the onset of content migration. Users may continue to access the content from the OLD website in read-only mode. There is no risk of new content being added to the OLD website during the transition.

Change management should also account for system down time (scheduled or otherwise). During times of system downtime, data redundancy often creeps in as users attempt to continue working throughout the downtime window. Determine how you will address this and document it as part of your Maintenance Plan.

## Disaster Readiness

Perhaps one of the most important sections of your Maintenance Plan describes a path for overcoming disasters. While your Disaster Preparation and Recovery Plan should be documented in your Governance Plan, Disaster Preparation should also exist within your Maintenance Plan to ensure all necessary components remain in place and operational.

The Disaster Preparation section of your Maintenance Plan should describe possible situations such as complete server farm loss, partial server farm loss, SQL server failure, network failure, intrusion (prevention and reaction), unexplained data loss, and associated steps required to get the system back online in a timely fashion.

Time estimates should be included in any Disaster Plans because the first question everyone will have is "How long will it be down?" You should have accurate estimates because you've *tested the recovery* regularly, right?

Your Maintenance Plan will include your schedule for disaster recovery testing. Regularly restoring your backups onto a testing environment will ensure the backups are working properly, and will help streamline the restoration process.

## Summary

Maintenance Plans do not need to be large complex documents, but ensure that they exist and have undergone proper thought, planning, and testing.

It is perfectly natural to not have all the answers as you get started. Just the act of writing the Maintenance Plan will surface potential issues which need to be addressed. This is yet another benefit of documenting your Maintenance Plan.

Stay in control of your **Site Collections** and Subsites to maintain organization and automate the removal of unused content. Plan your backup schedules and restoration procedures.

While updating metadata and tags is continual, schedule time to review and update your metadata annually as part of your formal **Taxonomy Evolution**.

**Search Tuning** is not fully automatic. Determine appropriate Crawl Schedules, and stay on top of what users are looking for and not finding.

Update the look and feel (UI) of your Site no more than once a year to ensure your Site remains fresh and relevant, and is following your organizations **branding** guidelines.

Plan, document, and test your **change management** procedures during content migration, configuration, customization, and system down times.

Finally, identify how your org will react to system failures and **regularly test your backups**.

# SharePoint for Public-facing Websites

Web Content Management (WCM), also referred to as a Content Management System (CMS), is perhaps the most underutilized capability of SharePoint. Your org can use SharePoint for the creation, management, support, and sharing of your public-facing website(s).

One SharePoint environment can support multiple public-facing website URLs such as your org Site, foundation Site, a dedicated annual conference Site, a dedicated community Site. On the other hand, these could all be components of a single, top-level URL.

Public-facing websites can be open to everyone and can allow anonymous users. These Sites can also have "members only" content, Pages, blogs, videos, downloads, etc. In the past few years, orgs have also started supporting "registered users" who fall between members and anonymous users. Typically in such scenarios, a person can create a new account (register) on the website to receive access to more information and functionality.

Before we delve into the specific SharePoint tools which enable WCM, we should describe a high-level methodology for planning and implementing a public-facing website.

This methodology is simple and has five stages: Discovery, Design, Technical Planning, Implementation, and Assessment.

# Discovery

The Discovery stage is used to identify and clarify the objectives and audiences of your public-facing website.

## Objectives

Begin your website solution design with high-level business objectives. These objectives must support your org's strategy. This sounds like common sense, but you would be shocked how many initiatives skip this crucial step.

We'll go out on a limb and say your website has only a couple of high-level objectives: **Education** and **Revenue**. If we were to use traditional business terminology, we could state your website supports Content, Commerce, and Community (though for many orgs community is largely about education).

Your website serves to educate your audiences at various levels. What are the issues your org is involved with? What is your org doing related to these issues? Is your website aggregating relevant information from all appropriate sources, including external sources? Does your website focus on professional development, credentials, certification, or personal development? Do you provide information not available elsewhere? Does your org provide analyses, standards, expertise, commentaries, subscriptions, or other products? Does it facilitate knowledge sharing between likeminded individuals?

Your website is also used to generate revenue. Before you cringe in disgust, realize we are referring to Membership, Event

Registrations, Subscriptions, Donations, Bookstore sales, Advertising, Career Centers, Conferences, and any other revenue-generating activity your org focuses on.

As you begin your WCM project, you should clearly articulate your objectives. Remember to Capture, Clarify, and *Confirm* these objectives.

## Audiences

Your website is built for them – not you. Your website is for your audiences. Your org likely has many audiences: anonymous public, or logged in members, volunteers, donors – everyone that supports your organization. Your website may be for students, teachers, educators, the press, government officials, affiliates, and other orgs. Again, your website is for them – not you.

It's for them to learn about you. It's for them to communicate with you. It's for them to communicate with each other – about you. It's for them to learn, contribute, teach, and share. Your website must serve many masters, but the master it should serve first and foremost is *them.*

Clearly define your core audiences. Just because your website is public-facing does not mean the entire world is your audience. Your defined target audiences will dictate your content, functionality, presentation, marketing, and structure.

Remember *they* will use the website only if it is convenient for them. They will use your website only if they can find what they want, when they want. They will use your website only if it works for them on whatever device they happen to be using when they find it.

Your users do not care about your technology. They don't care about your AMS, CRM, CMS, Financial Package, servers, widgets, or ACME parts.

Your users do care about you. They care about your content. They care about the Page, the file, the audio, and the video. They care about what you say, and they might care even more about what the other users say on your website. They either want *Content*, *Commerce*, or *Community*.

## Content

What content do you have today? What format is it? Do you have HTML pages, PDF files, videos, and podcasts? Is it all in one location, or is it spread out all over the place? Is it in a CMS already?

It is never too early to perform a content audit. A content audit should actually be an ongoing effort of your org. You should have a handle on your content and the way it is managed. The sad reality is most orgs don't. The content audit can seem overwhelming, but it really is a simple task which just happens to be time consuming.

Content is king, has been king, and will continue to be king for the foreseeable future. If your website has irrelevant or just bad content, your website will not be successful.

In most cases, your top-level website content is actually marketing copy. Put your salesperson hat on when you write your content. On your website, your content is one of your products. Your audiences are your customers. Think about how to sell your product to your customers.

Train your staff how to write better content for your website. Have a genuine interest in providing the best possible content for your audience(s).

# Design

Design is more than just pretty pictures. Design is the entire user experience (UX) and user interface (UI). In fact, the pretty pictures should be the last part of your design stage. You should first define the structure and usability, and then make it pretty.

### Contextual Planning

Plan the entire design in the context of SharePoint. SharePoint provides a lot of capability right off the shelf. While SharePoint can be molded programmatically to be anything you need, that doesn't mean it should be.

Remember to start with configuration and resist customization. Leverage the power provided out of the box as much as possible.

Your planning team needs to be aware of SharePoint capabilities. They need to see it in action and be able to use it. They need a sandbox so they can try ideas during the design stage. Remember,

SharePoint provides a lot of configurability through in-browser configuration. Use it.

## Wireframes

Wireframes are the best way to plan the logical layout of individual Page templates. The technology you use to develop a wireframe can be pencil and paper or software. Wireframes should be done before any artwork or creative design. The wireframe should be kept simple, but should serve these very important purposes:

> - Suggest the overall structure of the website.

> - Suggest the relationship among Pages.

> - Suggest the relationship among areas on a single Page.

> - Suggest the necessary templates that will be used throughout the website.

> - Suggest the global and secondary navigation.

Wireframes can be used for initial usability testing, link prediction testing, and most importantly, for communicating website and Page structure.

## Navigation

Your users should be able to find your content. They need to be able to browse through an intuitive navigation structure and find the content they are looking for.

SharePoint provides two tools for managing navigation. First is a Navigation manager. This tool makes it very easy for an authorized user to update the navigation.

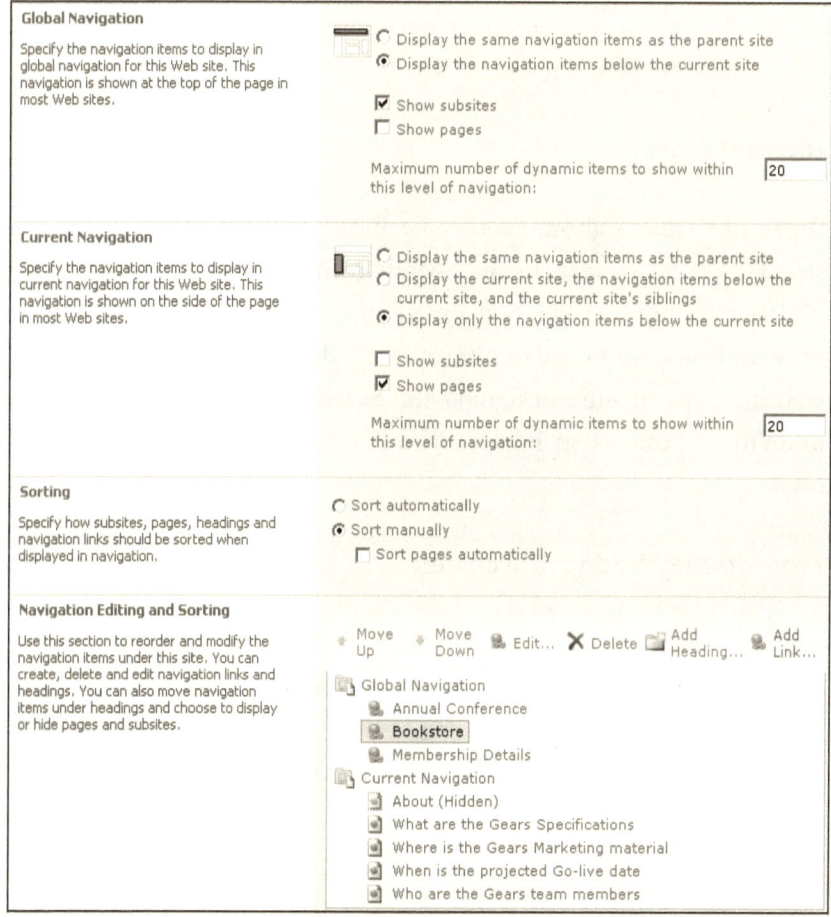

**SharePoint Navigation Management**

Navigation should not be static. Continuously revisit and update your navigation based upon the behavior of your users. If new trends appear that demand significant attention; your users should be able to easily browse to that content.

Second, metadata driven navigation provides users with the ability to rapidly browse and discover information in Document Libraries using metadata filtering and views.

## Internal Search

We're not talking about Google or Bing. We are talking about the search box on your website. Search comes with SharePoint. It is not an afterthought or a bolt-on solution. Search is an integral part of SharePoint, and needs to be an integral part of your public-facing website. Spend time designing the Search experience. Define the usability. Search is so important we've dedicated an entire chapter on it.

## How do they find your website?

We *are* talking about Google and Bing here. Search Engine Optimization (SEO) is the art of optimizing your site and your content to ensure that search engines list your site as the top results for particular searches. SEO drives users to your site to find you.

Here are seven high-level steps to ensuring your SharePoint public-facing website is ready for the Internet search engines.

## SEO Step 1: Search Terms

Make a list of the search terms you want people to find your website with. Start with the broadest terms and then get more specific. These should be terms which describe the overall theme of the site.

## SEO Step 2: Competition

Identify and research your competition. Your competitors include any site which ranks in the first ten slots using the above search terms. Now that you have identified your competition, it's time to research. Determine the keyword density of the page which is ranked well.

Keyword density is the percentage of times a keyword or phrase appears on a web page compared to the total number of words on the page. You do not want to publish a page with a keyword density much greater than the site which is ranked number one. You want your pages keyword density to pretty much mimic it. How long have they been around? What exactly do they offer and why do people go to their site? Basically, you are sizing them up to see what you are up against. Document these findings for each search term in your list.

## SEO Step 3: Analysis

Analyze your website. For each search term, identify which page is most suited or relevant. Determine its keyword density, and add or subtract content accordingly. Again, you want to have about the same keyword density as the page ranked number one. Always tailor your content for users, not search engines. Once your page is ranked within the top positions, you can almost forget about keyword density and focus on fresh theme, relevant content.

## SEO Step 4: Confirmation

Ensure your website is being crawled. This can be determined by searching for your domain name. If it's not automatically being crawled by a particular search engine, manually submit your site. Do not pay a so-called "SEO" company (online or otherwise) to submit your site to "thousands of internet search engines." Use some good old common sense on this one – how many search engines really matter? Hint: you care about the ones you have actually heard of, which is likely something less than "thousands."

## SEO Step 5: Site Map

A SiteMap is a way to describe the Pages of your Site to a search engine. It also provides the mechanism for letting search engines know when your Pages have been added, removed or modified. A SiteMap file is an XML formatted file containing an entry for each Page of your Site. Each entry contains the date/time the Page was last modified.

There is a unified "SiteMaps protocol" used by the big three internet search engines (Google, Bing, and Yahoo!). This means one SiteMap file can be used by all three major internet search engines.

Create a sitemap.xml file, register it with the major search engines, and keep it up to date. Keeping the sitemap.xml file up to date can be a daunting task with even the smallest of websites. For this reason, it is recommended that you automate this process. You want your sitemap.xml file to be updated every time a page is published/approved as well as moved, removed or otherwise modified.

## SEO Step 6: Links

Secure quality in-bound links to your site. These links should come from sites that are theme relevant and ranked better than your website pages. Do not participate in "link exchange programs", or other shady short-cuts. Pick up the phone and make some calls after figuring out what you can offer in return. You want the in-bound link to originate from text describing the page on your website it is linking to, which should be the relevant search term. More quality in-bound links equal higher rankings.

## SEO Step 7: Monitoring

Keep watching your rankings and continue adding fresh content. Continue trying to secure quality in-bound links to relevant pages. Do not get frustrated and try to cut corners, you will undoubtedly regret it, especially if your website gets blacklisted. Mostly, continue tailoring your content for your intended audiences. Proper SharePoint WCM site SEO is handled at the page level, not the site level. In other words, let your content authors do their jobs and ensure they understand the rules.

Regardless of how they arrive at your Site, there are several features are important to your website users.

## Mobile Device Support

We have iPhones. Our parents have BlackBerries. Many of your users will visit your site at some point with a mobile device. While mobile browsing is significantly better than it used to be, consideration should still be given to the mobile experience.

SharePoint has native support for mobile browsing. Lists, Libraries, and Web Part pages all have native mobile views that are configurable. SharePoint supports personalized mobile views which allow your power users to determine what they need to display on their individual mobile views.

How much time and effort should you spend on the mobile experience? It depends. In order to make this decision, you really need to understand your audience and your metrics.

A good place to start would be to determine how many mobile visitors your Site currently receives. This information is located in your website logs, Google Analytics, WebTrends, or whatever package you are using today. If you don't have analytics, install Google Analytics. It's free, takes a few minutes, and in the next few weeks you'll at least have some metrics.

Trend this data across the past 18 months to infer some basic predictive forecasting. At what rate are mobile users increasing? What will this number look like 12 months from now?

What are mobile users looking at? How long do they stick around? At what page are they most likely to exit the site? This information will help you determine which areas of your site need special mobile attention, and which are fine with native SharePoint mobile compatibility.

## Related Content

Consider this. A user is on your site reading an article about how a federal government regulation change affects them. Wouldn't it be great if your website did what the Amazon.com website does? Based on the article you are looking at, here are some other articles that you may find interesting. Here are some products we sell that you may find interesting. Here are some upcoming events which you may be interested in. This is accomplished using SharePoint metadata, and it is easy to display related content.

## Integration

Facebook, Twitter, LinkedIn, YouTube, Conference Site, AMS, CRM, and any other property or system that falls within your ecosystem might need integration (or might need to be integrated). The question becomes: What level of integration, and why?

Why do you want to integrate your website with Facebook? What's the business objective? How does this objective serve the overall mission of your org? Ask the same questions about every integration: Why and What?

Provide a simple way to share your content on Facebook, LinkedIn, and Twitter. Make it easy to locate these social media assets from any page of your website.

This can easily be done with free services such as ShareThis.com or AddThis.com. Do not reinvent the wheel by using custom development to achieve this goal. Make it easy and keep it simple.

**Social Bookmarking**

## Content Rating

Users care more about what your other users think about your content than about what you think about your content. The ability to see what everyone else rates as the best content on your site makes it easy for them to determine which content is likely to be worth consuming.

Video, audio, PDF, PowerPoint files, and web content are all capable of being rated with SharePoint. Rating content is actually a gateway drug into broader interaction and participation. People like to passively chime in, so let them. Before you know it, they might even be an active participant in your member community!

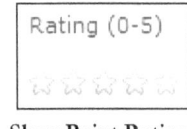

**SharePoint Rating**

## Comments

It's easy to rate content as four stars, but comments are more important than Content Rating. Users prefer to see comments from other users with descriptive information – not just a rating. Nonetheless, ratings are still important as the vast majority of users will not participate in a commenting system.

Commenting allows discussions to take place at exactly the right time and place. SharePoint 2010 provides full commenting using the Note Board.

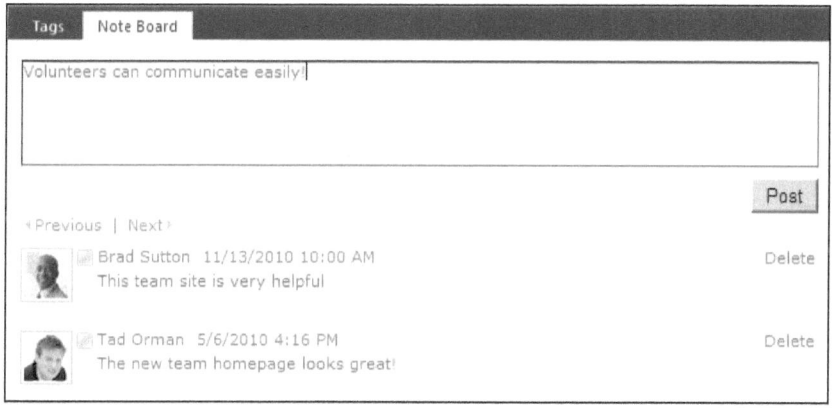

**SharePoint Note Board**

## Branding

The user interface is important to all audiences. Previous versions of SharePoint really fell down if you didn't use Internet Explorer. Microsoft adopted global web standards (not Microsoft standards) with SharePoint 2010, and it looks great on all modern browsers.

SharePoint supports a template approach for applying user interface consistency across your site. Branding begins at the top level with a Master Page. The Master Page is the global template through which content will be displayed in.

A typical Master Page will define the header, footer, global navigation, and sometimes the right and left navigation, depending upon the design you have chosen. The Master Page generally includes references to your cascading style sheets (CSS) and any global scripting Libraries that you may be using (such as JQuery).

In addition to the Master Page, SharePoint supports Themes. Themes are a way to change the basic style components without changing the physical layout of the content.

Themes change the font, font sizes, text colors, link colors, calendar colors, and default navigation colors. Themes are useful to designate different site areas (departments, silos, chapters, committees, etc.) without changing the overall user experience.

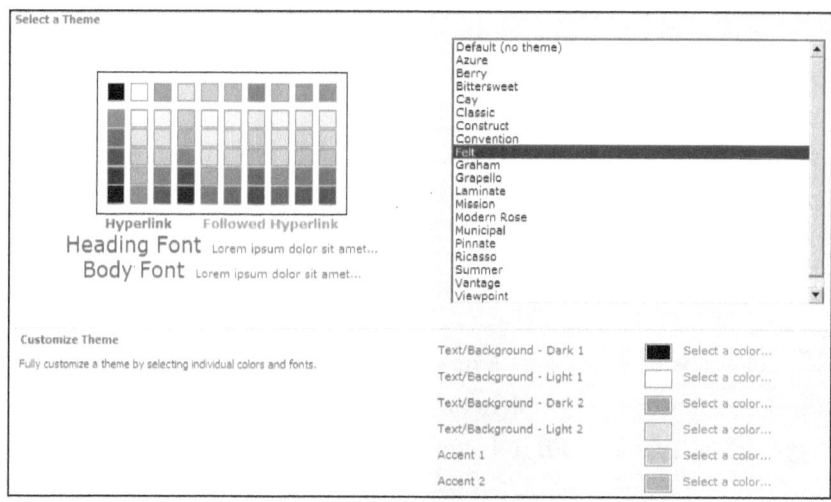

**SharePoint Themes**

## Accessibility

SharePoint 2010 supports published accessibility guidelines (Section 508 compliance) and conforms to the W3C WCAG guidelines. Some orgs have strict requirements for compliance due to federal funding, but for most orgs, it is a strong desire and not a requirement. SharePoint 2010 ships with compliance so it's a non-issue.

## Consistency

Any user should be able to determine how to get around your site and find what they need, regardless of what page they are on. Users deep link directly into your site from Google, Bing, and your Search engine.

Navigation needs to be clear and concise. The grouping of your content needs to make sense to them (not you).

Your various web properties need to have a global branding. Your entire ecosystem should be consistent. Everything you broadcast to the world should be easily identifiable as your brand. All of your web assets should have your orgs "feel."

If your website user clicks a link to an article on your magazine site, the branding or color scheme can change, but the entire user experience (navigation, UI, search location, taxonomy, feedback tools, etc.) should not change. The user needs a familiar and consistent interface in order to experience a sense of location.

SharePoint supports consistency, within and across websites, with templates. Utilize SharePoint Site Templates and Page Layouts to preserve consistency.

## Technical Planning

The technical planning stage defines the how. How is the site going to be constructed? How exactly will it be managed? Which Site Templates will be used? How will Workflow, Search, Taxonomy, Content Types, Audience Targeting, and Site Columns be used? How will SharePoint be used?

Technical planning also defines the *system boundaries*. SharePoint does not exist in a vacuum. It will have integration points. It may connect to your network, your membership database, CRM, AMS, financial system, job board, subscription site, commerce site, or any number of other systems.

Define system boundaries. Define which systems will do what. Define what SharePoint will do and not do.

For example, you may already store all of your user information in your AMS or CRM. You may already have a membership database where you store your user profile details. Continue storing all relevant user information in your database. Store your usernames, passwords, addresses, email accounts, demographic information, expertise, product purchases, event registrations, and all other user information in your membership database. All of your member information will be in a central location. This simplifies your marketing, analysis, and reporting.

Do not limit your membership database to only members. All of your registered users should be in the same membership database. Community users, donors, volunteers, and members should all be in the same database with different (or multiple) designations.

The technical planning stage should provide at least the following:

➢ Plan for configuration of all SharePoint components

➢ Plan for any required customizations

➢ Plan for integrations like authentication and ecommerce

➢ Plan for Single Sign On details

➢ Plan for implementation management

➢ Plan the work breakdown of all tasks

# Implementation

Finally, you can start construction. You could have started building earlier in the process, but you should now see that planning needs to be a priority.

A single username and password should grant your site users access to all of your properties through a Single Sign On (SSO) mechanism. A user should be able to authenticate one time in one location, and be granted (or denied) access to various site features based upon their roles and status. SharePoint provides a framework to leverage your existing usernames and passwords.

SharePoint provides a mechanism to leverage existing roles. If the membership database/CRM/AMS already has designations for membership levels, committees, councils, or any other working groups, SharePoint can leverage those "Roles" to associate with security.

SharePoint may be integrated with other business systems using the Business Connectivity Services (BCS). The BCS functionality is one of the most powerful features of the entire SharePoint platform.

BCS allows a business user (you really don't have to know how to write code) to define an external database and use that data within your SharePoint site. You can use the BCS to display information from a Membership Database, or to display your products, event details, member profile details, financial information, order processing details, and any other data which you have access to in a backend database system – whether you are hosting it yourself or not.

## Assessment

Review, analyze, benchmark, and revisit. Think of the website as a living, breathing organism which exists in the complex ecosystem that is your org. Assessment should be an ongoing exercise.

Continuously improve your website. Improve the content, structure, design, and capability. Roll out new features and continuously give users reasons to revisit your website.

## SharePoint WCM

Hopefully you now understand how to implement a successful pubic-facing website project. Now we'll review some of the features which make SharePoint a solid choice as a CMS platform.

### Browser-based content management

Content authors (staff, volunteers, bloggers, and web gurus) are able to use a browser to create and manage content. They are not tied to a desktop tool.

Content authors are able to update your website from the road, from a hotel, from a phone, and from an iPad. They can create and edit content in SharePoint from a browser.

### Browse and Edit

Publishing content on a SharePoint website is similar to typing a Microsoft Word document and clicking the save button. Many CMS systems require content authors to go to an administrative area behind the curtain to manage content. In SharePoint, content authors simply browse to the page they need to work with.

Content authors will see things non-authors will not see, like the Edit Page link. Authors can type new text, format existing text or paste content (including pictures) right into the page. SharePoint will cleanse and format the content to match the rest of the site.

The interface has an uncanny resemblance to Microsoft Word. Content authors who are familiar with Word should feel right at home using the SharePoint interface to work with and manage content on your website.

## Familiar Editing Interface

Any recent WCM solution has a WYSIWYG (What You See Is What You Get) editor. SharePoint takes that a step further and provides an editing interface similar to the Microsoft Office Ribbon.

**Familiar Editing Interface**

Content authors can see what the Page is going to look like in the context of navigation and design as they are authoring and editing the Page.

No single web page exists in isolation. Every page created is in the context of the website with other Pages, videos, images, Comments, Ratings, etc…

## Distributed content authoring

SharePoint allows content authoring and publishing from anywhere with complete accountability and transparency. Allowing multiple people to create and publish content is not a technology barrier. It's a business process decision about how your org creates, manages, and publishes content to the website.

Many orgs utilize SharePoint's built in Workflow to automate the review and approve processes associated with publishing content to the website. Typically, multiple people will create content for your website. Content should go through the appropriate approval process and ultimately get published on your Site. Authoring, editing, and approving content involves multiple people working on many different Pages simultaneously, and should be managed automatically using Workflow.

## Easily define roles

SharePoint lets you add an individual a role that you've created. Define roles for content authoring, editing, and publishing different types of content. Do not assign permissions to individuals. Assign permissions to a role, like "Communications."

Perhaps your communications guru will be promoted to CEO and no longer be the one managing the website every day. You need an easy way to give the next communications guru the same permissions that the first one had. Just add the new guru to the same role. Voila! The new person in the role can now do EVERYTHING on the website that the other person was doing last week.

## Workflow

Workflow is the automation of a business process. Orgs use SharePoint workflows to automate the review and approval process of website content. The activities could be updates, approvals, validations, email notifications, status changes, or any number of processes you wish to automate.

Some workflows need to be time based. Perhaps if a particular web Page is old, it's time to update it or remove it. SharePoint Workflow may send the author of the Page an email reminding her to update the Page.

Some workflows need to be person based. For example, one particular content author needs their manager to approve the Page before it goes live.

Some workflows should be content based. For example, the annual report needs three levels of approval before it goes out to the board of directors.

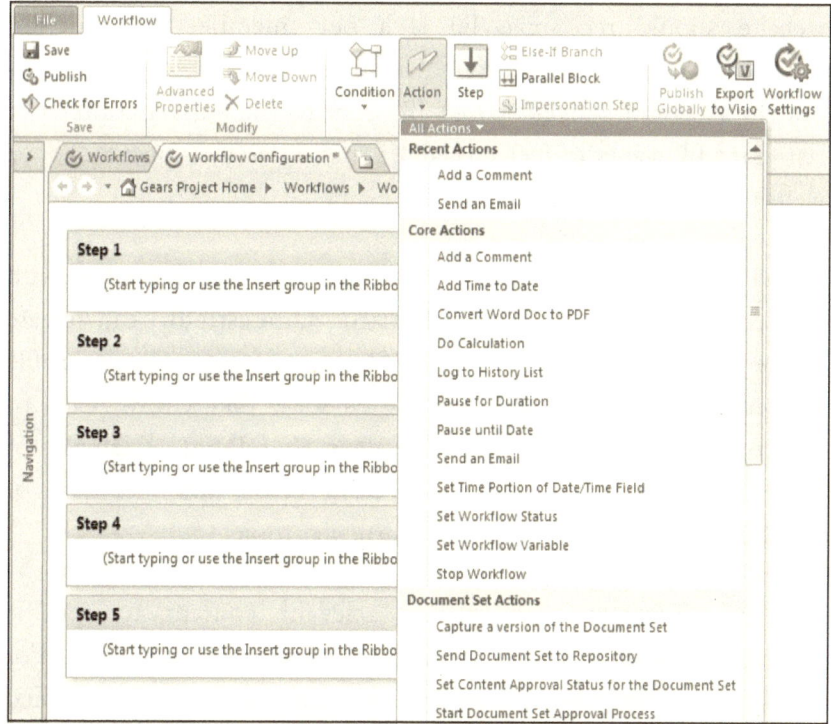

**SharePoint Designer 2010 Workflow Configuration**

SharePoint workflows can be configured by a business user – **not a developer**. It's easy to create new workflows, update workflows, review workflows, and even copy existing workflows.

## Personalization

SharePoint uses Audience Targeting as one way to introduce personalization and targeting. An Audience is a SharePoint term for a subset of your authenticated users.

Your website should recognize Jill Member and offer something of value to Jill. Jill logs in and expects a personalized experience. Your website should recognize Jill is a new member or that Jill's membership is about to expire. It should be able to see that Jill bought a certain widget or that Jill went to the annual conference last year. Jill wants to feel special. Jill has come to expect that your website will treat her as such.

SharePoint satisfies these types of website requirements with Audience Targeting. An authorized administrator can create Audiences based upon user profile properties. These profile properties can map to your existing database (like CRM, AMS, or AD) or you can add properties directly in SharePoint. Examples of Audiences may include: members from Texas, new members, or anyone expressing an interest in a particular topic.

Audience Targeting can surface relevant content to specific Audiences. Web Parts can leverage Audience Targeting. For example, you can create a new web page about the benefits of going to this year's annual conference. You can then 'target' this page to any user who went to last year's conference but has not yet registered for this year's conference.

## Analytics

Who is using the site? How are they using the site? What pages are popular? Where are they coming from? How long are they staying?

SharePoint provides these analytics – including search usage analytics. What are they searching for? What are they NOT finding?

You can also use Google Analytics, or other third-party package simply by inserting the tracking code in the SharePoint Master Page.

## Templates

Everything in SharePoint starts with a template: Page Layouts, Site Templates, Document Templates, Workflow Templates. In fact, the initial SharePoint Site itself is based upon a template provided by Microsoft.

## Multilingual

Many orgs have a need for their website to support multiple languages. SharePoint provides multilingual support. SharePoint Language Packs also provide the administrative components in multiple languages (not many CMSs offer this capability).

Variations are used in SharePoint to represent multiple versions of content in different languages. If you want your website to be available in Arabic, Chinese, French, Spanish, and English, Variations allows you to create, link, and manage the content in each of these languages (and more).

To be clear – SharePoint does not TRANSLATE your content automagically into another language. If you have ever used automatic language translation software, you already know it's not the way to go. SharePoint supports multiple Variations of a page for each of the languages that you wish to support. Your org may have an About Us page in English. Variations allow your site to support the About Us Page in any other language that you wish.

SharePoint also has out of the box Workflows that support translation management. If your content author creates a version of a page in English, SharePoint can assign that page to your Spanish translator for conversion to Spanish.

The translator would then key in the Spanish version of the Page which would then be the Spanish Variation of that page. Many orgs rely on translation service companies to perform the translation. In this case, SharePoint can be used to automate the process of packaging the content, sending it to the translation service company, and receiving the translated content back.

## Should SharePoint be your CMS?

SharePoint provides a lot of features that make it a great choice to run your public-facing website(s). Does that mean it is the perfect fit for everyone? No.

### Product versus Platform

SharePoint is a platform. Sure, SharePoint is a product that Microsoft makes, but SharePoint is a platform that can be used to construct solutions of all kinds. This means it's capable of being more than the sum of its parts – which makes it infinitely more powerful than a single purpose CMS. It is capable of so much more than "just a website."

Orgs use SharePoint for their public-facing websites; and have logins to their SharePoint-based member community, a place rich with content and interaction which really drives home the orgs' value proposition.

Orgs use SharePoint's blogging capabilities, wikis, discussion boards, search center, ratings, comments, newsfeeds, and email- and SMS-based notifications. They use the RSS capabilities, dashboards, calendars, announcements, content scheduling, personalization, and content targeting.

Orgs use SharePoint workflows to automate content review as well as approval cycles, event registrations, and submitted abstracts. They integrate SharePoint with their membership databases and keep track of metrics like conference attendance, renewal rates and subscriptions.

Orgs use SharePoint to surface information from external data sources like AMS and accounting systems. They mix and match capabilities from a seemingly endless pool of possibilities; and they do this without developers ever being involved, using the familiar Microsoft Office interface.

SharePoint is much more than just a CMS.

**Is SharePoint ever a bad fit?**

Maybe? There are some things SharePoint doesn't do well, and some things SharePoint doesn't do at all.

SharePoint is not ecommerce. SharePoint can integrate with an ecommerce system, but it is not ecommerce in itself. Most orgs will use their existing AMS or CRM to provide commerce, so this isn't a big deal. Microsoft provides a solution that integrates SharePoint with Microsoft Commerce Server for ecommerce purposes.

SharePoint is not an email marketing tool. The AMS or CRM software typically provides email marketing. SharePoint can integrate with other third-party email marketing tools (in fact, Commerce Server has email marketing). Many orgs use SharePoint to compile specific email lists based on user profiles, user site usage, and other factors. These lists are used by their email marketing solution which tracks bounce backs, click-throughs, spam alerts, etc... but SharePoint is not email marketing.

## Summary

SharePoint is a Web Content Management **platform** with enormous potential for supporting many of your org's objectives, including your website. Because SharePoint is a platform, orgs mix and match features to best satisfy their website requirements. SharePoint has too many features to list in a summary. We commonly see orgs utilizing many of these features for their public-facing websites and member communities of all types.

SharePoint has powerful and user friendly ways for authoring your website. SharePoint is **search engine friendly**. Proper implementation and SEO discipline can achieve search result rankings with Google, Bing, and Yahoo. Keeping the readers' attention is up to your content authors, and SharePoint can't help you write interesting things. SharePoint does, however, make it very **easy to publish** interesting content to your website.

**Multilingual features** support website content and administration in multiple languages. Preserve consistency using **templates**: Page Layouts, List Templates and Site Templates.

**Analytics** provide tools to track and report on trending information related to basic website analytics. Use **Advanced Analytics** to track and report on sophisticated usage related data such as "who's doing what, when and where" (at least on your website).

**Personalization** targets the right content to the right users using tags and SharePoint Audiences.

**Workflow** automates business processes such as Page review and approval cycle. Define **roles** that honor existing AMS or membership database roles. Author content from anywhere with **distributed content authoring**.

Embed **videos** on your website or member community by dragging and dropping them from a video Asset Library.

Create and edit content using a **browser-based content management** interface which mimics Microsoft Word with full WYSIWYG capabilities.

Allow users to experience a top-notch **search** experience with the powerful SharePoint Search algorithm and related capabilities. Integrate and surface information from your AMS, membership database, or any other third-party business systems with **Business Connectivity Services**.

Allow users to post **comments** on articles, videos, images or any other content located on your website or member community. Allow users to start participating by **rating** your content. Display related articles, videos, podcasts, or any other **related content** from SharePoint or external systems.

SharePoint supports all major browsers including **mobile device** based browsers. Provide a consistent **user interface** experience using master pages and templates. Easily manage your website **navigation** to keep it highly useful and user friendly.

# SharePoint for Your Staff

We have come to expect Web 2.0 and Social features as part of our everyday collaborative lives. Your employees expect the same. Social features are just the latest of collaborative advancements which will continue to improve as ideas fuel technology. Finding information quickly coupled with communication will continue to drive this advancement.

SharePoint makes it easier for people to work together. Working together. That is the goal, right?

We all want to work more efficiently *and* more effectively. We all work with other people. Working together is what it's all about. Collaboration has become quite a popular buzzword, and the word collaborate literally means to work together.

How does SharePoint make it easier for your hard working staff to work together, to collaborate? SharePoint provides the medium on which you can easily share your stuff, and others can share their stuff with you!

You can replace the word "stuff" with any number of specific substitutes: content, documents, slides, files, calendars, contacts, tasks, projects, workspaces, images, videos, audio files, spreadsheets, and so on.

## What is an Intranet?

An intranet is a private computer network used for securely sharing any part of an organization's information within that same organization. By definition, your staff collaboration will take place within your intranet.

In many cases, SharePoint serves as an intranet. It's your org's place to share stuff with other staff users. If you plan on allowing members, donors, volunteers, or other non-staff groups access to your intranet, don't. *Intranets* are intended only for staff users. Period.

Allowing non-staff users access to your intranet (on a large scale) undermines the very definition itself as well as the security model used to keep internal data secure.

Non-staff users such as members and donors belong in your *extranet*. Let's look at how your association or nonprofit can effectively use SharePoint to achieve streamlined staff collaboration within the context of your *intranet*.

## Work Management

Work management can be broken down and represented as the following scenarios:

➤ **Personal** Work Management (your own stuff)

➤ **Team** Work Management (teams within same department)

➤ **Department** Work Management (your department's stuff)

➤ **Project** Work Management (across multiple departments)

Notice three of the four work management scenarios consist of teams working together. Enter SharePoint.

SharePoint can be used by individuals and teams to share information, to co-author documents, to automate business processes via workflow, and to organize and track knowledge. Remember that SharePoint can be used to create, aggregate, prioritize, recommend, and deliver content.

This is accomplished by using different SharePoint components. Your understanding of the various SharePoint components will determine the usefulness of your staff-facing intranet.

Security is paramount within the context of an intranet solution. You need to ensure that outsiders (non-staff users) do not gain access to your internal data. It's equally important to ensure internal staff users can gain access to your intranet, but only see what they should see. SharePoint manages this with ease, but it requires careful planning.

Give careful consideration to the availability of your intranet. Will you allow authenticated access across the internet? Will you publish the site using SSL? Will you require a VPN connection?

While it does not work for all orgs, our personal opinion is to make your intranet accessible to your users from any device. Publish your intranet website on the internet using SSL and require authentication. Enable your users to collaborate and do not provide unnecessary obstacles.

The structure of your SharePoint-based intranet site should follow Information Architecture (IA) best practices. This essentially means ensuring your content is easily findable by your audience, which in this case is your staff. Your intranet site structure may closely resemble the way your organization is structured.

## Sample Intranet Site Structure

You may have an intranet site structure similar to the following:

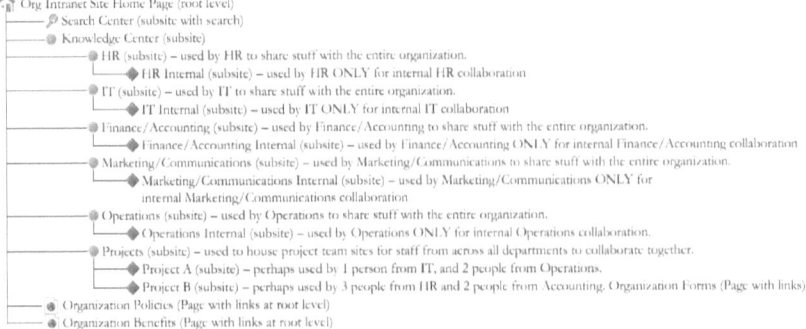

**Sample Intranet Site Structure**

You can see this structure may grow quickly. And keep growing. That's precisely why it is important to plan your site structure in a manner that not only accommodates your present requirements but also allows for manageable scalability according to your Governance Plan.

The structure of your intranet site is expected to change over time. This is important. Your intranet should grow and change. Your org is not static. Your org changes over time (sometimes overnight), and your intranet should change with your org.

Within each Subsite, you will have the ability to leverage all the powerful collaboration features that SharePoint has to offer. Just because you can do something does not necessarily mean you should.

For many orgs, it is better to identify the immediate must-haves and roll-out new features on a planned schedule. This approach will not only keep things fresh but will also minimize the sometimes overwhelming effect SharePoint can have on your users.

## Sharing within Teams

Team collaboration features are often utilized within a team specific Subsite. You can think of Subsites as sections of your intranet. You may have a need for a "Project A" Subsite to house all artifacts related to Project A. Permissions may be granted at the Subsite level to provide proper collaboration abilities to the appropriate individuals.

It would probably make sense to give all users who are actively involved with Project A appropriate permissions within the Project A Subsite to add, update, and delete documents. However, that does not mean those same users should have those permissions throughout the entire intranet.

Generally, users will not have the same permission levels across the board. Users within the HR department will not likely have *add* or *modify* permissions within the IT Subsite.

The following are some commonly used SharePoint solutions as they relate to Team and Department Work Management

## Workspaces

A Workspace is a Subsite. Technically speaking, a Workspace is a SharePoint Site built from a Site Template. A Workspace is a place to temporarily or permanently work on and share things like Documents, Tasks, Calendars, Contact Lists, media files, and more.

Document Workspaces are Subsites designated for the collaboration of one or more documents. Event Workspaces are Subsites designated for the collaboration around a particular calendar event, like a Board of Directors meeting, your Annual Meeting, or even specific committee meetings. Workspaces are often created for the temporary collaboration around a specific document or event, and later discarded or archived after the finalized output is achieved.

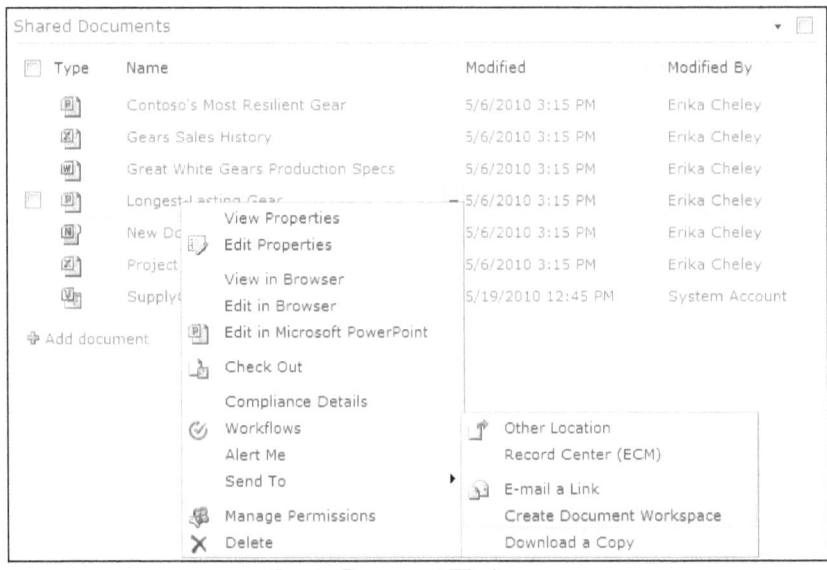

**Create Document Workspace**

# Document Management

Of the collaboration features and capabilities available within SharePoint, the Document Management capabilities are the most heavily utilized.

## Document Libraries

A Document Library (Doc Lib) is a container used to store files. These files may be any file types you wish (PDF, MS Word, Excel, PowerPoint, TXT, etc.). The SharePoint Administrator can set file size restrictions as well as file type restrictions. You may have as many or as few Document Libraries as you need.

Permissions can be set on a Document Library to control who *has* access and who does not. You can set permissions to restrict specific users to "Read Only", while other users may have full control to add, update, or delete files. Workflows may also be configured at the Document Library level to ensure that all files contained within the Library are subject to the workflow rules.

## Document Check-in/Check-out

A user can Check-Out a file (or multiple files) for editing to ensure that other users cannot edit the file at the same time and override their changes. When a file is Checked-Out, other users can easily see whom the file is checked-out to. Additionally, other users can still open and read a checked-out file; they just can't save their changes.

*Note*: SharePoint 2010 offers Co-Authoring when used with Microsoft Office 2010. Co-Authoring is simultaneous document editing. In short, you can open and edit a Word 2010 Document; meanwhile others can edit the same document at the same time. The application shows you where others are making their edits within the document, and you will be able to see their actual changes when they save the document. For this to work, the Microsoft Office 2010 Document must live in a SharePoint 2010 Document Library.

## Document Versioning

Gone are the days of "filename_org_annualmeeting_2010-6-14_v3.doc". Thank goodness! Emailing the same document to multiple people and requesting feedback is painful at best. While it's easy to receive a document, open it, make some changes, and send it back – the person on the other end now has to manually aggregate everyone's changes together, and likely send the document again for final review. This is inefficient.

With SharePoint, you can send a link to the Document. Users click the link, Check-Out the document, make changes, and Check-In the Document. A new Version of the Document is created in the background every time a user performs a Check-In. This virtual paper trail continues so you can easily go back and compare Versions, and even restore a previous Version as needed. The best part is that you can eliminate confusing and inefficient versioning in the file names. Some of your users don't even follow the naming conventions that you've setup. You know who they are.

## Document Workflows

Automating your business process can save lots of time, paper, and greatly reduce human error. In a few clicks, you can create a Workflow to route a Document through a review and approval process to all the right people and in the right order.

Workflows can range from basic (as just described) to sophisticated. The creation of sophisticated workflows requires the help of an educated SharePoint Designer 2010 user or developer. Basic workflows can be easily created using a browser in the SharePoint web interface.

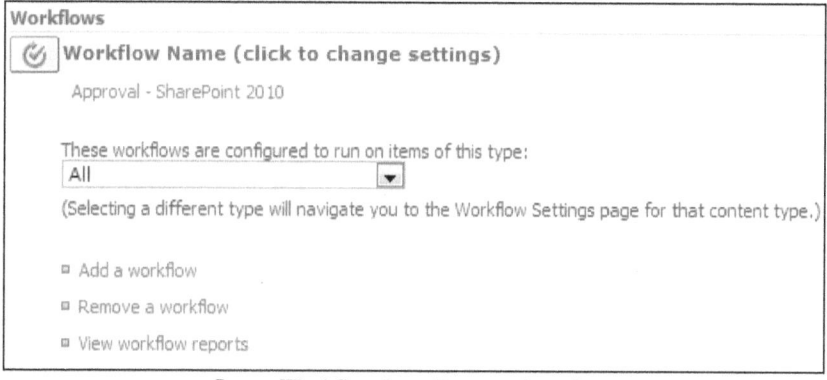

**Create Workflow from Browser Interface**

Many Document Workflows end up being a basic review and approve process. This process may be a serial process whereby each step of the workflow occurs in sequence, or a parallel process whereby multiple people review and approve simultaneously. This just depends on your specific business processes.

**Manage Workflows from SharePoint Designer**

# Task List

Not just a clever name, a Task List is used for assigning and tracking Tasks. Tasks may be re-assigned and prioritized. Users can also work with SharePoint Task Lists from within Microsoft Outlook. Updating Tasks directly in Outlook 2007 or above will automatically update the associated Tasks in SharePoint.

| Title | Assigned To | Status | Priority |
|---|---|---|---|
| Review Sponsorship Guidelines | Jim Stover | Not Started | (2) Normal |
| Finalize Keynote Contract | Josh Bordner | Not Started | (2) Normal |
| Launch Registration Portal | Brad Collins | Not Started | (2) Normal |
| Schedule the Room | | In Progress | (2) Normal |

**SharePoint Task List**

# Calendars

SharePoint Calendars may also be controlled from within Microsoft Outlook. SharePoint 2010 Calendars may be setup to display events from multiple Calendars. A common intranet scenario is for each department to have their own "Department Vacation Calendar." You may also create a calendar in SharePoint called "Global Vacation Calendar" which overlays all department calendars onto one view so you can easily see who's on vacation across the board. Event Workspaces may be created for any event on any calendar.

**SharePoint View of Multiple Calendars**

# Contacts List

A Contacts List is a common and important function within an intranet. The Contacts List is not intended to replace your AMS or CRM for your org, but you can effectively use a Contacts List to manage contact information for vendors, partners, members of the press, or government contacts.

SharePoint's Contact Lists may also be integrated with Microsoft Outlook. This will allow staff to quickly locate contact info from either Outlook or the SharePoint interface.

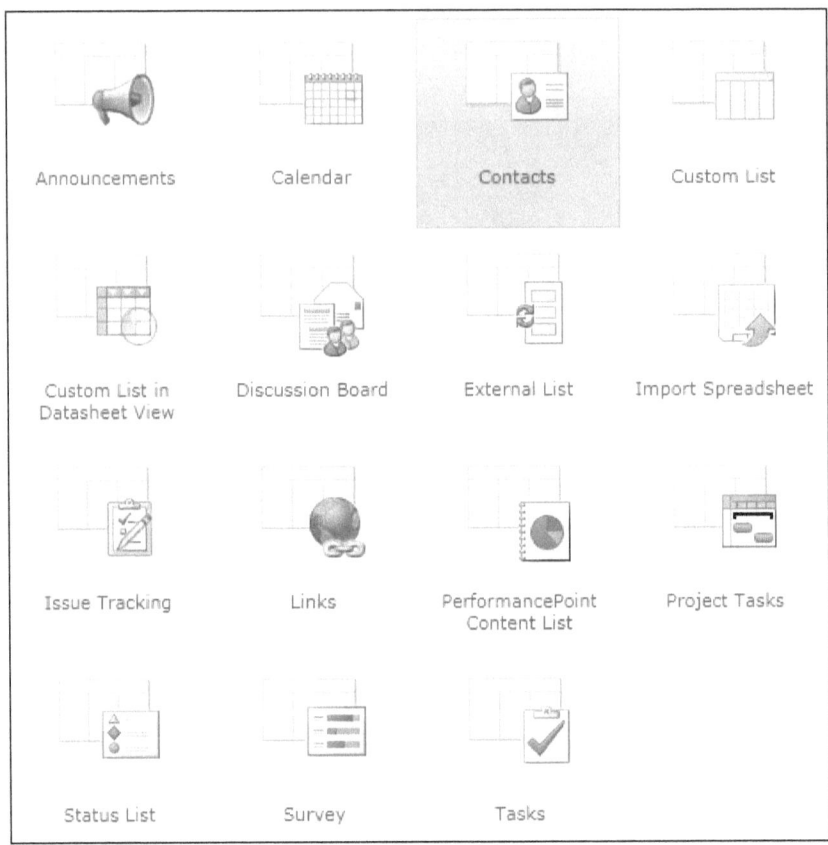

**Create Contacts List**

## Asset Library

Media such as audio or video files should be stored in a SharePoint 2010 Asset Library. An Asset Library is a specialized Document Library designed to make working with digital media assets easier.

SharePoint 2010 introduces new technology to stream audio and video without requiring costly and cumbersome third-party solutions. The Media Player Web Part goes hand-in-hand with your

Asset Library. The Media Player Web Part can easily be configured to play videos contained in your Asset Libraries, making it easy for any of your authorized users to embed audio or video on your pages.

One of the best uses of media that we've seen for intranets is to provide training videos for staff. Orgs have written countless pages of documentation describing how to manage websites, upload files, and perform any of the hundreds of standard operating procedures (SOP) within the org. We have seen great success using one- to five-minute videos to actually show users how to perform tasks.

Using any of the low-cost or free screen recording software packages, you can create timely training videos that show your users EXACTLY how to use your systems – including SharePoint. Record a single 60-second video that shows your users how to Check-Out a Document on *your* site – not a vanilla SharePoint site. This takes very little effort to record and upload. With very little time or money invested, you can have a very robust training section of the website that shows bite-sized chunks of exactly how to do very specific activities. Your users will love it.

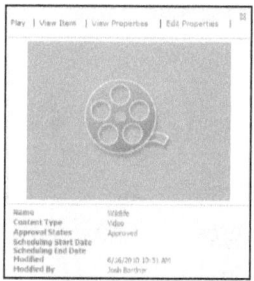

**SharePoint Media Player Web Part**

## My Site and Personal Site Features

If you recall, Personal Work Management was the only work management item not directly correlated with team collaboration. Users need a personal space to house their own files, documents, bookmarks, notes, tags, images, etc. Users need a place to keep and manage their own stuff.

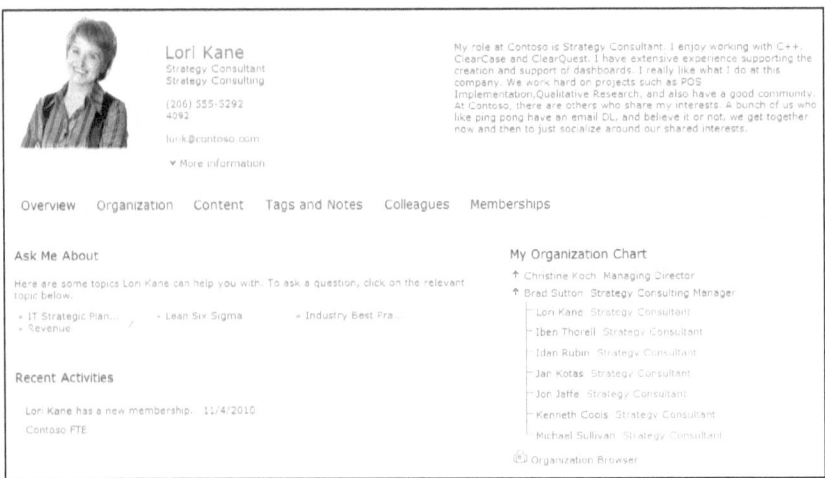

**Personal Work Management with SharePoint My Site**

That's where the SharePoint My Sites comes in. My Sites are more than just a virtual drive. My Sites provide the interface for users to keep Profiles updated. The Profile contains information about the user, and (optionally) allows them to determine who gets to see what details. The Profile stores more than name and contact information. It can store user education, information, project involvement details, interests, anniversaries, birthdays, and other information you wish to store about your users.

The SharePoint My Site is where your users store files. There are so many horror stories about corrupted drives, stolen or lost laptops, and misplaced files. It does not make sense to have a laptop or desktop as the only location for any information.

The My Site is part of the SharePoint website environment. This means you can access My Sites from any computer with proper user credentials. You can rest assured your My Site content is being properly backed up.

Users can also share files with Colleagues from their very own My Site.

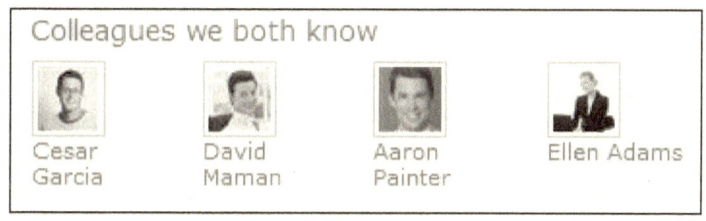

**Colleagues**

The SharePoint My Site is also where professional networking happens, making your org smarter. For example, you can write on someone's Note Board. This should not to be confused with the Facebook Wall. Though you might as well call it their wall, it behaves in a similar fashion.

You can tag things throughout the intranet and view your tags from your My Site. You can tag any content stored in SharePoint: Documents, Pages and Items – anything in SharePoint. You can also tag websites outside of SharePoint using Internet Explorer.

You can view how other people have tagged content as well. You can follow certain activities such as ratings, profile updates, tags, and more. This is "Facebook for your org". These social features add a new degree of communication, interaction, and collaboration capabilities for your staff to utilize.

My Sites sound pretty fantastic, right? My Sites are only available with the paid versions of SharePoint. In other words, My Sites are not available with SharePoint Foundation (the free one).

## Summary

SharePoint allows your staff users to store, share, and collaborate on any type of content easily. Content can be documents, slides, files, calendars, contacts, tasks, projects, workspaces, images, videos, audio files, spreadsheets, or any other data or information being created or consumed.

SharePoint provides an array of collaborative and document management capabilities which can be used to maximize staff efficiency and overall organizational effectiveness. Understanding these capabilities and associated best practices will ensure your intranet solution has a broad user adoption and minimal overhead.

By definition, an **intranet is for staff users only**. Use an extranet to collaborate or publish content to non-staff users like members, supporters, donors, or volunteers. Do *not* use your intranet.

**Work Management** can be logically separated into personal work, team work, and departmental work. Structure your SharePoint intranet site to support all these scenarios.

SharePoint Workgroup Sites can be used for **cross-departmental collaboration** which is a form of Team Work.

**My Site** and Personal Site Features provide the medium for users to store and work alone, work with others, and keep profile information current.

Web 2.0 and social features are now expected and are largely perceived as collaboration mechanisms.

# Supporters, Members, Volunteers, and Donors

Supporters come in all shapes and sizes, but we're really focusing on members, volunteers, and donors. For many charities and nonprofits, volunteers are the life blood of the organization. For associations, members are often the primary audience. Whether someone chooses to volunteer their time or their money, this external support is critical for orgs all over the world. Technology is an integral part of each of these groups' ability to engage your org on a regular and efficient basis.

You need to make sure that your supporters can find you! Increasing traffic to your Site using Search Engine Optimization (SEO) is extremely important. If no one can find your website, then it really doesn't matter what technology you have in place.

Once your supporters have found you, they want to engage. In the past, it was enough for an org to just have static content on their website. Now the status quo is much higher. Engagement is the new expectation. Your supporters expect to be able to immediately contribute. Contribute money, ideas, thoughts, videos, comments, or ratings.

Engagement is a two-way street. Not only do your supporters expect to be able to contribute to your org, but they expect to be able to *interact* with you. Your supporters also expect to be able to interact with your other supporters. This idea is not new. In fact, community is one of the core principles behind many orgs. Your technology must support your *entire* community. It's both your community and your supporters' community.

## Build a Successful Community

Building a *successful* community requires a *strategic social strategy*. The ingredients are simple, yet are often overlooked. Your strategy needs to answer some important questions which will ultimately determine the success of your community:

> ➤ Who are your audience members?

> ➤ What's in this website that is important to *them* that cannot be found elsewhere?

> ➤ Is this *the* place where they _____?

> ➤ What's in it for them (members, volunteers, public, etc.)?

> ➤ What's in it for your org?

The interesting thing about a member community is you have the ability to *ensure* it's a success.

**Simply providing users with a URL and some Web 2.0 and social features will fail as a community.**

Your strategy should include a methodology for success. Follow this methodology to ensure a thriving, successful, and sustainable member community.

Choreograph the launch of your new community. Socialize the idea with your supporters and staff prior to launch. Your users should be excited about the launch date. Send out teaser emails leading up to the launch. Send out announcements such as "4 Days till Launch!" or "See you soon online!"

Within the community Site itself, things need to be happening! Content must be created daily. Your community website needs to be the place for panel discussions and where new presentations are first posted. It should not just be a place to get data.

Assess the assets available to you. Determine what data and content you have to offer like videos, presentations, papers, audio, podcasts, industry news, membership directory, reports, etc. Utilize staff talent at your org by identifying what they're passionate about and encouraging them to express this passion in the community.

Perhaps a fellow employee is ALWAYS talking about current legislation. Ask this person to write a blog in the community. Give them a few hours a week for new posts. Give them TIME to contribute to the community.

Empower as many *passionate* people as you can within your community. Passion is the difference between another boring website and an exciting and provocative experience!

Your org's active participation is vital to the success of the community. You wouldn't invite people to your home for a party and not show up yourself, would you?

A good host is always present. The active involvement of your org staff needs to initially be higher, but can taper down as active community leaders step to the forefront. This too should be planned, encouraged, and accounted for in your strategic social strategy.

Within your community website, it is extremely important to ensure questions get answered quickly. This is particularly critical when you first launch your community. For many people, asking a question is a risk. They are taking a risk and putting themselves out there.

It is absolutely necessary they get a response within a timely fashion. The quality of the actual response is not as important as the act of responding. This reassures them. This reassures everyone who sees the post. It lets them know the community is habitable, friendly, and not a desolate wasteland. Responding to posts is very important.

Managing the community will require time and effort. It takes time to answer questions. It takes time to find, create, and publish fresh content on the Site. Successful communities do not happen by mistake. Your strategy should account for the time involved with community management. The schedule planning portion of your strategy may resemble the following:

> ➢ 20-30 minutes each morning, afternoon and evening (daily)

> ➢ One hour each week uploading new content (videos, articles, podcasts, blog posts, news, etc.)

➢ Four hours each month for online events

➢ Four hours per month for a formal Community Newsletter

Time should also be scheduled for the tasks leading up to launch, such as socializing the idea of the new community. Plan well in advance for the launch and ongoing success of your community:

➢ The **first month** of your community is the babysitting stage and will require the most effort.

➢ **6-month action plan**. What new and exciting experiences can people look forward to?

➢ **12-month action plan**. Similar to 6-month but even better! This is a good time to show appreciation to your community ambassadors, and to the members who actively participate in discussions, blogs, comments, and answer questions. Your ambassadors should be formally acknowledged.

➢ **Measure success**. Plan regular analytic review sessions to identify needed improvements.

➢ **Improvements**. Plan time to make improvements on a regular basis.

Many orgs experience paralysis by analysis with a bad case of the What-Ifs. "What if someone says something bad about us?" or

"What if someone says something mean to someone else?" This list goes on.

The What-Ifs is a sad condition which has a cure. Planning is the cure. Your strategy should account for "Detractors." Detractors are how we address all those What-Ifs in a thoughtful manner. Simply create and populate a table containing the following column headings:

> ➢ What type of detractor?
> > Example: Legitimate complainer.

> ➢ Why they make trouble?
> > Example: Needs help with something or warning others.

> ➢ How do you recognize?
> > Example: Raises legitimate issue. May use strong language but seems open to reason.

> ➢ What you should do?
> > Example: Solve problems or explain policies; explain publicly or add to FAQ if possible.

Fill this table with every possible What-If you can imagine. You will be surprised how quickly fears related to the What-Ifs go away when they are written down and accounted for!

## Using SharePoint

As you may recall, Sites are one of the key building blocks within SharePoint. Sites provide a way to logically organize information based on content and security rights. For many orgs, it makes perfect sense to use a SharePoint Site for logical groups of users. Committees, Chapters, Councils, Boards, Volunteers, Volunteer Leaders, Teams, Scientists, and other Special Interest Groups can benefit from having dedicated SharePoint Sites.

Each Site provides a protected area for discussions, calendars, blogs, videos, document sharing, and any other collaborative activity your org wishes. The SharePoint Site can be private and only available to the group, or open to the entire community to view and contribute. Remember SharePoint Site Groups and Permissions? It's very easy to control who has access to what.

Don't let it stop with the formal groups which already exist in the organization. SharePoint Sites can be useful for certification classes, topics of interest, important government regulations, and other groups which are created every day within the org.

**Select a SharePoint Site Template**

Your supporters can create ad-hoc groups on LinkedIn and Facebook today. Why not give your supporters that same level of capability in your community? Why not embrace your community and be an active participant? After all, it's your community, too.

SharePoint natively supports a hierarchical structure of information using Sites. Within a top level URL, SharePoint lets authorized users create Subsites, or a Site created under another Site.

The Subsite could have distinct permissions or could inherit the permissions of the higher level Site. You can define the permission inheritance when creating the Site, but this can be changed at any time.

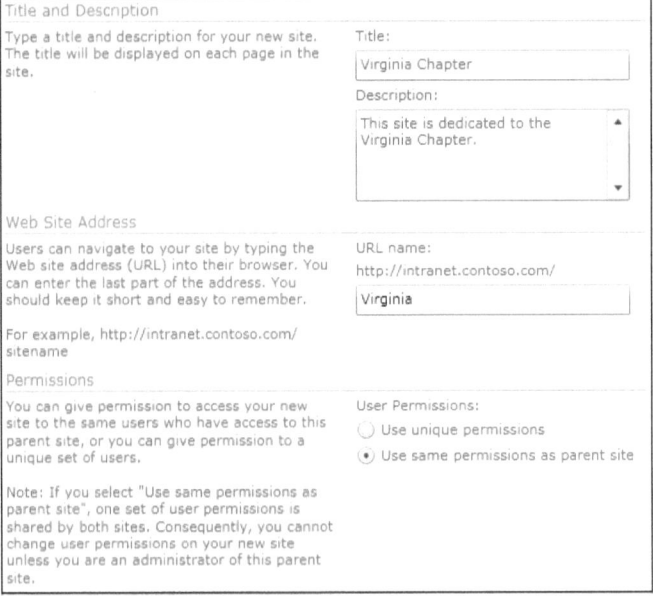

**Provide Information about the New Site**

You can create more than a single tier of Subsites. SharePoint supports a full hierarchy. You can create Sites under Sites under Sites under Sites… This is powerful not only from a content management and Information Architecture perspective, but also from a content aggregation and distribution perspective.

You can create entire ecosystems of Sites around particular topics. You can create Sites with Subsites about any topic or interest. Volunteers can be grouped under a single Site. Within that Site there could be various geographical Subsites, for example.

Volunteers can have their own micro-communities specific to their local Chapter or geography. These micro-communities can leverage Sites with their own local Calendars, Document Libraries, Task Lists, Issue Lists, registration forms, and member information.

Users can choose what to SHARE with other micro-communities and what to keep private. Best practices, training, knowledge, calendars, and FAQs can all be shared among volunteer groups to gain efficiencies, reuse templates, and promote education and understanding – all within your global community.

Using the concept of the hierarchical Sites, your org can support personalized and granular teams dedicated to a particular topic, interest, idea, geography, or other group that bonds individuals together. This concept is easy to grasp and implement through the use of a Site-based architecture.

Sites allow you to define sections that group content based on security (think Board of Directors) or based on content (think new volunteer orientation).

It may make sense for your org to utilize a top level Site to organize all Volunteer Orientation. This Site could have documents, blog posts, event details, videos, slide decks and various other types of content that relate to basic Volunteer Orientation.

A single Volunteer Orientation Site may make perfect sense for your org, but then someone points out that Volunteers from different countries need different training. What works in Canada does not work in the US. What works in China does not work in Mexico. Many of the guiding principles are the same, but there may be distinct details that are important for volunteers to understand within that particular country.

One solution could be separating the different countries into their own Subsites under the top-level Volunteer Orientation Site. This would allow both content distribution (top down) and content aggregation (bottom up). Aggregation could be used to surface information from the different country Subsites into the top level to share with all Volunteers.

## Content Aggregation

SharePoint provides tools that allow widely distributed content to be aggregated or rolled-up into a single location. This makes relevant content easier to find and utilize. One of the easiest ways to achieve content aggregation is through the Content Query Web Part (CQWP).

The CQWP is available in SharePoint 2010 Standard and Enterprise. The CQWP is a Web Part capable of aggregating nearly any type of content and displaying it in a single location. Items displayed by this Web Part are only displayed to users with proper permissions (Security Trimmed).

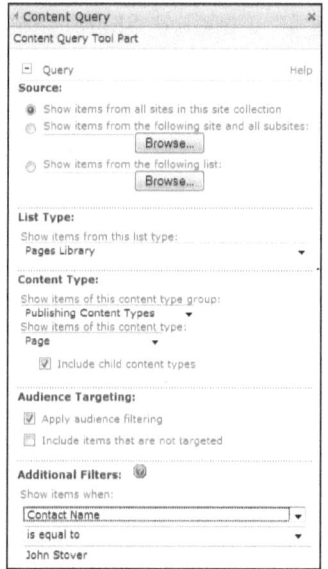

**Configure Content Query Web Part**

In the Volunteer Orientation example described above, each volunteer Site may have an FAQ. FAQs could be created by anyone. You may allow volunteers, administrators, staff, and educators to all submit FAQs at their local Site level.

The CQWP can aggregate all FAQs from the entire set of Sites and Subsites, then display them in a single display of global Volunteer FAQs. This promotes true distributed content authoring, managed locally within the org, and aggregated into a single global display.

## Content Distribution

Timely distribution of information is critical within any org. Announcements List is a native SharePoint List that can help distribute info throughout your org quite efficiently. The idea behind Announcements is simple: provide a simple way to display announcements to users of a Site. Announcements (by default) consist of three simple Columns: Title, Description, and Expiration Date.

Using the same Volunteer Orientation Sites as an example, a single Announcements List can be created at the top level of the global Site. The home page of the volunteer orientation Site could have a Web Part showing recent announcements. Ideally, every user would see the Announcements when they go to the global landing page.

In reality, users of the Site will bookmark their specific, localized home page deep within the Site structure. Canadian Volunteers will likely bookmark the Canadian area of the Volunteer Orientation Site since that's where they spend most of their time.

If they go directly to that page every time, they may never see the actual Announcement which you've created at the root level. Good news! You can use a Web Part to place ALL global announcements on each of the individual Subsites. Users would see all relevant announcements.

Write your content once and repurpose it for use throughout the entire ecosystem of Sites.

## Community Contribution

"Community" is a broad term which is perhaps over utilized. It is a hot buzzword in the nonprofit and association world right now.

Hopefully, you're starting to see how SharePoint can take the contribution of EVERYONE in your community and aggregate it for consumption by authorized users.

Thoughts, ideas, best practices, FAQs, documents, Templates, Surveys, Blog posts, Wiki entries, suggestions, questions, and even Ratings are all ways to crowd source the collective knowledge. Yes, even Ratings.

Which of these suggestions and ideas contributed to your org are good? Which ideas are great? You don't have to decide alone. Ratings make this possible for the community to become its own filter.

That brings us to another capability you should leverage in your communities. How are your volunteers using the Site? What are donors doing on your Site other than making a onetime donation?

## Templates

Templates are useful in all volunteer initiatives. Templates make it possible to standardize a Word document, a spreadsheet, a presentation, a web page, or an entire Subsite. In fact, when you install SharePoint, you are required to select a "Site Template" to be used for the very first Site you create.

One of the benefits of templates is consistent user experience. A common requirement of nonprofits with local fundraisers is to set and monitor attendance goals (and of course monetary goals). By providing templates, you can ensure data consistency. Consistency is retained throughout the reporting process. This will save a tremendous amount of staff time that would have been spent cleansing data.

This example could be achieved using a Microsoft Excel template. The individual running the event will download an Excel file, save the file locally, and then upload the file back into the system after filling it out. This is a popular choice because many people are comfortable using Excel. Your supporters likely already know how to update fields in Excel.

SharePoint, with its inherent Office integration, provides a way to pull data out of Excel. This provides consistency and data validation across all environments. Using templates also provides consistency for the volunteers and supporters in the field. The next time the person helps with an event, they will have the same type of experience.

Using File Templates are great, but there are other ways to leverage SharePoint to accomplish consistency. Perhaps you can a web-based form to capture data. Use a SharePoint list. This is much more lightweight, is customizable, and does not require downloading or uploading files.

Using a List allows the information to be entered directly using a browser. This information is immediately validated and submitted to the database. Another benefit of Lists is that your form and the captured data are available in a mobile device format, automatically.

# Analytics

Ask various people throughout the org on how community users are utilizing your Site, and you will likely get completely different answers from everyone. There is a scientific way to figure out how the Sites are being used (or not used). Analytics.

SharePoint has analytics tools built in, but are they enough? For most organizations, the provided analytics will be enough because few people will actually look at the analytics. This is a sad fact that is pervasive in many orgs. There are orgs which spare no expense to get the most comprehensive and most sophisticated analytical packages available; yet few make use of the advanced analytic capabilities.

SharePoint provides basic analytic tools. There is definitely room for improvement, but the tools that do exist are worth utilizing. There are three areas where you need to look at analytics: Site Usage, Search Analytics, and third-party analytics.

## Usage Analytics

First is traditional Site Usage Analytics. This is great for determining how many people are viewing a specific page of your community. See which pages are most popular. Determine where people are leaving your Site. Keep in mind analytics are only helpful if you actually do something with the information. For example: if you determine through analytics that a recent volunteer case study is popular, then highlight it on the main home page. Push additional traffic to the case study, write a blog post about it, and use the current popularity of the article to drive traffic.

A powerful way of determining *who* is doing *what* can be found in SharePoint Custom Audit Reports. Custom Audit Reports may be created by community administrators and shared with others. Custom Audit Reports provide valuable information about the behavior of your community members. These reports are specific.

For example, use Custom Audit Reports to see who has downloaded a particular PDF file. Orgs have successfully harvested this type of data and merged it with analytical data for predictive forecasting purposes. Remember that SharePoint has incredible business intelligence tools which can be leveraged against your analytics data.

You can now determine that users with a specific membership level, who read a particular article, *and* download a specific case study, have a 90% higher renewal rate than average members. Who cares, right? Your Marketing, Communications, and Membership departments care. Your CEO cares. Your Accounting and Finance team cares.

This type of intelligence is like gold to them! The information gleaned from this one simple example can be used to increase renewal rates, increase new memberships, improve budget forecasting accuracy, and make room for countless improvements.

## Search Analytics

The second area of analytics, deserving of even more focus, is Search Analytics. While the chapter on search provides more detail, it is important to realize Google has changed how people use your website. Website users simply expect your search box to deliver exactly what they are looking for, every time. They want to see a single text box for search. They expect to type in a single word or phrase. They expect to get what they want, right now. We all do.

Most users don't have the time or desire to try to guess their way through your navigation structure. They will jump directly to your search. In this case, traditional analytics are less helpful. Search analytics will provide much better insight by identifying the most popular search keywords. Search analytics will reveal whether content is buried too deep on your site, or whether users are searching for topics that are not on your Site. If you have popular content buried too deep in the Site, you should probably put links to it from other areas. If there are a lot of searches for content that you don't even have, should you?

## Third-Party Analytics

The third area of analytics you should focus on is third-party analytics such as Google Analytics (GA). We said it! Use Google Analytics. For starters, the price is right – Google is free. The time setting up a Google account and Google analytics, and then plugging in the analytics tracking JavaScript to your SharePoint page only takes minutes.

Here are the steps involved with using Google Analytics on your SharePoint site:

1.  Create Google Analytics account.

2.  Register your site with Google Analytics.

3.  Copy/Paste the Google generated code (just a few lines of JavaScript) into your Master Page.

This will give you great analytics which will map directly back with your campaigns in Google. You are using Google AdWords to drum up donors, volunteers, and members, aren't you?

A quick word of caution: Google Analytics is free and comes with all of the support of free software – very little. Google has lost several orgs' historical analytic data during system outages and crashes. It was painful, but it didn't kill them. They still have their SharePoint analytics after all.

While SharePoint may satisfy the technology requirements for a member community, you are still not across the finish line. It takes more than features and functionality for a member community to thrive and be sustainable. It takes more than technology to have a "successful" member community.

## Summary

SharePoint provides the functional capabilities required for highly collaborative communities. Your supporters, members, volunteers, and donors will not likely embrace these features unless you have carefully choreographed the solution.

A strategic social methodology is required to ensure an effective online community. SharePoint provides many of the applicable tools for building successful communities, but only if your org leverages SharePoint with a proper strategy and passionate engagement.

# SharePoint Licensing: Ain't Nothing Free

SharePoint 2010 is more powerful and easier to use than ever before, but how do you license SharePoint 2010? SharePoint can be hosted on premise (meaning you can host it yourself), hosted in a managed environment, or hosted directly with Microsoft as a SaaS offering. Regardless of where or how you choose to host your SharePoint environment, the licensing and product information is consistent.

**Disclaimer: We do not work for Microsoft or a software reseller. Discuss all of your licensing needs with a Microsoft Licensing Specialist or your software reseller/vendor.**

This information is intended to be used as a guide. Many resellers are quite unclear about licensing details and will usually err on the side of selling you more software than necessary.

Details regarding SharePoint 2010 prerequisites and SharePoint 2010 system requirements are crystal clear. SharePoint 2010 is 64-bit only, requires 64-bit Windows 2008 Server, and requires a few other components before installation can begin. Unlike prerequisites and installation details, SharePoint 2010 licensing is still a mystery for many people.

## Microsoft SharePoint Foundation 2010

SharePoint Foundation 2010 is the next logical version of what used to be called Windows SharePoint Services (WSS). Had Microsoft continued with the previous naming convention, then

273

this product would have presumably been called WSS 4.0. SharePoint Foundation 2010 is a free addition for Windows 2008 Server. This is an important note: SharePoint Foundation 2010 is free. Windows 2008 Server is not free. You must have appropriate licensing for Windows 2008 Server to run SharePoint Foundation 2010. That said, you can utilize Microsoft SharePoint Foundation 2010 to run many different types of Sites: internal Sites, external Sites, departmental Sites, and even public-facing anonymous Sites. To be perfectly clear – you can run an anonymous Site on SharePoint Foundation 2010, you just need to have the appropriate Windows 2008 Server licenses. Download SharePoint Foundation 2010 directly from Microsoft.com.

## Microsoft SharePoint Server 2010

As with Foundation, Microsoft changed the name of this product as well. The previous version was called Microsoft Office SharePoint Server 2007. The latest version is called Microsoft SharePoint Server 2010. Notice the omission of the word "Office" from the SharePoint product title. The rumor is that dropping the word "Office" was an attempt to clarify that Office is not a requirement to run SharePoint. While SharePoint works spectacularly with Office, there are hundreds of SharePoint solutions that do not require or utilize any type of Office client.

There are two distinct license models for SharePoint Server 2010 – one for internal deployments and one for external deployments. Internal and external deployments are defined by "who" accesses the SharePoint environments. If SharePoint is being accessed by org staff only, then it is defined as internal.

Internal SharePoint environments require a Microsoft SharePoint Server 2010 server license with the appropriate SharePoint 2010 Client Access Licenses (CAL).

If the SharePoint farm is being accessed by "non-staff", including anonymous users through a public-facing website, then it is defined as external. External SharePoint deployments require SharePoint 2010 for Internet Sites licensing. Both internal and external license models are available for both Standard and Enterprise editions. Refer to "Three Card Monte - SharePoint Versions" for an explanation of versions and respective differences.

**Staff Use**

SharePoint Server 2010 is licensed in a traditional client/server model. The SharePoint Server 2010 server license is required for every server in the SharePoint farm regardless of whether the server is physical or virtual. Whether you have a single server farm or a multi-server farm, each server must have a SharePoint Server 2010 server license.

The client portion consists of the SharePoint 2010 CAL. Like other Microsoft CALs, you can purchase either *user* or *device* SharePoint 2010 CALs. User CALs are the most common; they authenticate each named user from any device they choose to use (mobile, laptop, desktop, etc.). The device CAL is used more commonly at locations with fixed workstations such as libraries, school labs, factories, or hospitals. The device CAL allows any number of users to authenticate, but only from the licensed devices.

There are two SharePoint Server 2010 CALs – Standard and Enterprise. The SharePoint Server 2010 CALs are additive. This means that in order to get the Enterprise features, you must purchase both the Standard CAL and the Enterprise CAL. You don't have the luxury of only buying an Enterprise CAL.

In an org where users will access Standard features and where a subset of users will utilize Enterprise features, you can purchase the additive Enterprise CALs for users who will actually be accessing the Enterprise features.

Note: Using security settings, you can configure the environment to ensure that Enterprise features are not being accessed by Standard licensed users.

## Non-Staff Use

The *external* license model consists of two products:

➢ SharePoint Server 2010 for Internet Sites Standard

➢ SharePoint Server 2010 for Internet Sites Enterprise

As described above, the 'for Internet Sites' are for "non-staff" Sites, such as public-facing, external, anonymous Sites. These licenses cover all forms of non-staff users even if those users are authenticating such as members, volunteers, and donors.

The Standard and Enterprise licensing models for Internet Sites provide the same functionality as the internal client/server CAL model counterparts. There is one additional consideration with the

SharePoint Server 2010 for Internet Sites Standard Edition. Standard will only support a single, top level domain and related subdomains (such as microsoft.org, communities.microsoft.org, blog.microsoft.org, volunteers.microsoft.org, etc.). The Enterprise version of Internet Sites has no limit to the number of top level domains that may be used.

### Internet Sites and CALs

No CALs are required for users licensed through SharePoint Server 2010 for Internet Sites. There are no CALs available for this licensing model. The Internet Sites licensing model is for external users only. Internal users are covered under this license only if all content, information and applications are also accessible to external users. Content authors, editors and managers are covered under this license as well.

### Mix it up

You can mix licensing models on the same instance of SharePoint, but you have to purchase both sets of licenses. Server and CAL licensing is not required for SharePoint users in order to manage information that is accessible to external users. Server plus CAL licensing is specifically required if you create a Site, Subsite, application, List or Library for *staff use only*.

## Windows Server

Windows Server is left out of many SharePoint 2010 licensing discussions. It is vitally important when determining the overall cost for any SharePoint 2010 initiative. You cannot run SharePoint 2010 without Windows Server.

SharePoint 2010 will only run on Windows. All versions of SharePoint 2010 are 64-bit, so you need a 64-bit version of Windows. SharePoint 2010 requires either Windows Server 2008 or Windows Server 2008 R2 (and presumably later versions). SharePoint 2010 is supported on the following Windows versions:

➢ Windows Server 2008 Standard (or R2)

➢ Windows Server 2008 Enterprise (or R2)

➢ Windows Server 2008 Datacenter (or R2)

➢ Windows Server 2008 Web Server (or R2)

Licensing for Windows Server 2008 follows the same basic principles with the client/server CAL model or the internet license. If you are licensing for staff users, Windows follows a client/server CAL model. Microsoft has details about the CAL model on the Windows Server 2008 Licensing Client Access License page.

If you are licensing for external users, then you need a Windows 2008 Server External Connector license. Microsoft also provides a detailed explanation of the External Connector license on their 2008 Licensing External Connector Licensing Overview page.

There are two exceptions that can work in your favor. You don't need CALs for up to two (2) Windows Server Admins. The other exception is that you don't need CALs if you are using the

Windows Server 2008 Web Server edition. This specific Windows Server edition is ideal for many orgs due to the cost effectiveness of implementation.

Regardless of the version of SharePoint 2010 that you are running, you must have Windows licensed appropriately. Your staff users will have CALs (user or device), and external users will be covered by External Connector licensed access.

## SQL Server

SharePoint requires SQL Server. SQL Server is the database that stores all the content SharePoint uses. The architecture that Microsoft has with SharePoint and SQL Server provides a scalable and flexible solution that can be scaled to multiple servers multiple SharePoint Servers and multiple SQL Servers. A SharePoint environment can also be configured as a single server running a free version of SharePoint (SharePoint Foundation) and a free version of SQL Server (SQL Server 2008 Express). Regardless of the configuration, SharePoint requires SQL Server. Due to the 64-bit requirements of SharePoint, you must also have 64-bit version of SQL Server, just like Windows. You can actually run any of a variety of SQL Server versions:

➤ Microsoft SQL Server 2005 64-bit with Service Pack 3

➤ Microsoft SQL Server 2008 64-bit

➤ Microsoft SQL Server 2008 R2 64-bit

> ➤ Microsoft SQL Server 2008 Express (only supported in standalone server configuration)

From a licensing perspective, SQL Server is the most flexible of all of the Microsoft software discussed in this series. There are more supported versions with more licensing options.

SQL Server has two main licensing models: client/server (CAL) and Processor Licensing. SQL Server is different than Windows or SharePoint when it comes to licensing.

You can choose either licensing model for either internal or external use. If your organization has so many end users that the Processor Licensing is less expensive to run internally, you can choose to run Processor Licensing internally (however, if you have a lot of SQL Servers you may find this model gets expensive quickly). On the flip side, if your external audience (authenticated users) is small enough, you can simply purchase enough SQL Server CALs to cover all users who will be authenticating into SharePoint 2010.

If you are running a public-facing website that does not require authentication (anonymous users), then you must utilize SQL Server Processor Licenses. SQL Server Processor Licenses are defined per physical processor – not per processor core. You can have a single, multi-core processor on your server (physical or virtual) and leverage a single SQL Server Processor License.

**Other SQL Server Notes**

Passive failover support servers do not require licenses as long as these servers do not have more processors than the active nodes.

If you are running SQL Server to support your SharePoint 2010 environment for public-facing websites, you must also purchase Windows 2008 Server External Connector licenses for your SQL Servers as well. Microsoft explicitly states that External Connector licenses should be acquired for each Windows server that the external user is accessing (not just for the server to which they are authenticating).

We've seen orgs try to avoid multiple SQL Server CAL licenses by insisting that users never connect directly to SQL Server because they connect through SharePoint. Microsoft explicitly defines these types of applications as multiplexing architectures, and further explicitly requires appropriate licensing for all users (or devices) that connect through any pooling, transaction, or multiplexing device, application, or appliance.

SQL Server 2008 Express is absolutely free, though it's scaled for simpler applications. Hardcore IT and SQL junkies would never advise you to launch a production application on SQL Server 2008 Express. Don't be intimidated. There are hundreds and even thousands of production SharePoint sites running on SQL Express – though appropriately sized and utilized. Here is a quote directly from Microsoft's SQL Server Licensing Overview: *"SQL Server 2008 Express edition is the fastest way for developers and enthusiasts to learn, build, and deploy simple data driven applications."*

## Microsoft SharePoint Designer 2010

SharePoint Designer 2010 (SPD) is a client tool in the sense that Microsoft Outlook is a client tool: it is installed locally on your laptop. SPD is specifically designed to manage SharePoint 2010

Sites, Lists, Libraries, Workflow, CSS files, Master Pages, Page Layouts, External Content Types, External Data Sources, and more. SPD is **free** and can be downloaded directly from Microsoft.

## Microsoft Search Server Express 2010

SharePoint Server 2010 comes with robust search capabilities. Microsoft Search Server Express 2010 provides the power of SharePoint Search for **free**. Microsoft provides a Search Server Express 2010 vs. SharePoint Server 2010 Search comparison that provides a very good, high-level overview of the differences.

Why would you use Search Server Express 2010? Maybe your org can't afford SharePoint Server 2010 in this year's budget. Maybe you are running SharePoint Foundation 2010 and want an enterprise search and not just the site level search. Maybe you want a powerful search engine to index your public-facing web site even if you aren't using SharePoint for your WCM. Maybe you want to search your file shares, Exchange public folders and other SharePoint sites, or even structured content in your database (like CRM/AMS/LOB systems). Maybe the most important reason to use Microsoft Search Server Express 2010 is because it's free.

## FAST Search Server 2010 for SharePoint

FAST Search Server 2010 for SharePoint adds even more functionality to the search capabilities of SharePoint Server 2010 Standard Search, including support for indexing up to a BILLION content Items, sub-second query latency, better search refinements, visual cues for rapid recognition (think thumbnail previews), advanced content processing, intelligent automatic metadata recognition, and much more.

FAST Search Server 2010 for SharePoint is included in SharePoint Server 2010 for Internet Sites Enterprise licensing. Microsoft provides a SKU to add a FAST Search Server 2010 for SharePoint license to your SharePoint Server 2010 License for your internal (client/server CAL) SharePoint Server 2010 environment. Here is a quote directly from Microsoft's SharePoint Licensing Details page, *"SharePoint Server 2010 for Internet Sites, Enterprise, also includes the rights to FAST Search Server for use in Internet or Extranet scenarios. You can deploy a single server license of SharePoint Server 2010 for Internet Sites, Enterprise, as SharePoint server or a FAST Search server—but not both concurrently."*

A wonderful resource regarding FAST is the FAST Search Server 2010 for SharePoint Evaluation Guide.

## Microsoft Office Web Applications 2010

Office Web Apps are the online version of Word, Excel, PowerPoint and OneNote so that you can access, view, and edit documents from any authorized web browser – PC, Mac, or mobile. Office Web Apps will run on any version of SharePoint 2010. Users are licensed through the Microsoft Office 2010 Volume License. This is Office licensing and not SharePoint licensing.

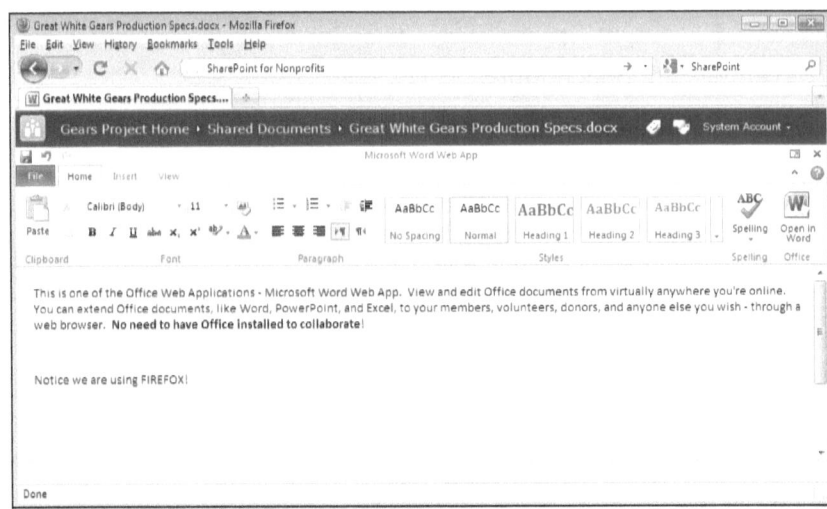

**SharePoint Office Web Apps**

# Microsoft Project Server 2010

Does SharePoint work with Microsoft Project? The short answer is yes. You can absolutely use SharePoint to manage MPP files including version history, exclusive check-out, workflow, alerts – just like any document type. SharePoint also has the ability to synchronize tasks with Project files.

However, you may have more demanding project management requirements. You may want to use Project Server 2010 to manage projects, tasks, durations, work breakdowns and assignments; or expose detailed project information to let other project team members view and update the information directly from their browser. Project Server 2010 is actually built on top of SharePoint 2010, providing a seamless integrated web experience, and allowing cohesive interaction with your entire project team.

Microsoft Project Server 2010 follows the same client/server licensing model as SharePoint Server 2010 for internal users. A server license is required for each server, and a Microsoft Project Server 2010 Client Access License (CAL) is required for each user that will authenticate and utilize the software. Keep in mind that Project Server 2010 runs on top of SharePoint Server 2010, therefore you must have appropriate licensing for SharePoint Server 2010 with both the Standard CAL and Enterprise CAL, and then add Project Server licensing. Depending on your configuration within an enterprise environment, the licensing required for *each user* may include:

> Project Server CAL (note that Microsoft Project Professional 2010 also includes a Project Server 2010 CAL)

> SharePoint Standard CAL

> SharePoint Enterprise CAL

> SQL Server CAL

> Windows Server CAL

For full details, visit Microsoft to obtain the Project Server 2010 Licensing Guide.

## What licenses do I need? Example Scenarios

These example scenarios detail the products which you will need to purchase specific to SharePoint 2010. For simplicity, these scenarios are limited to Windows, SQL, and SharePoint licenses.

These examples do not include antivirus software, backup software, management software, or any other ITC-type software packages.

### Scenario A – SharePoint Foundation Intranet

Org wants an intranet site for 20 staff using SharePoint Foundation 2010 single Stand Alone Server.

This would be a single server configuration running only SharePoint Foundation 2010 on the included SQL Server 2008 Express (which would automatically be installed during the SharePoint Foundation install).

> ➤ One (1) Windows Server 2008 Standard

> ➤ Twenty (20) Windows Server 2008 CALs

That's it! All you need is Windows Server and appropriate CALs for your users. If you have an existing Windows shop, you likely already have the Windows CALs. Then all you would need is another Windows Server. You could consider running SharePoint 2010 on an existing, under-utilized server and thus would not need to purchase any new licenses to install and run SharePoint.

### Scenario B – SharePoint Foundation Public-facing Website

Org wants to launch a public-facing (Internet) website running SharePoint Foundation 2010.

Public-facing website assumes anonymous access and the sites are not for staff only. This could be an Extranet, working with clients, vendors, customers, members, volunteers, or any other non-staff. Similar to Scenario A, this environment uses single server as a standalone server. Remember for non-staff or internet-facing sites, you don't need any CALs.

- ➤ One (1) Windows Server 2008 Standard

- ➤ One (1) Windows Server 2008 External Connector

## Scenario C - SharePoint Server 2010 Intranet

Org wants an intranet site for 20 staff using SharePoint Server 2010 single Stand Alone Server.

Consider this a small Intranet site running on a standalone server. All employees will be using Standard Edition functionality. This is a single server configuration running only SharePoint Server 2010, Standard, with the included SQL Server 2008 Express.

- ➤ One (1) Windows Server 2008  R2 Standard

- ➤ Twenty (20) Windows Server 2008 CALs

- ➤ One (1) SharePoint Server 2010, Standard

- ➤ Twenty (20) SharePoint 2010 CALs, Standard

## Scenario D - SharePoint Server 2010 Intranet Site

Org wants an intranet site for 20 staff using SharePoint Server 2010 in a two (2) server configuration.

This would be a two-server farm, with a web server running SharePoint Server 2010 and a database server running SQL Server 2008 (or 2005). For this sample configuration, all 20 employees will utilize SharePoint 2010 Standard features. In addition, only 10 of these 20 employees will utilize SharePoint 2010 Enterprise features.

➤ Two (2) Windows Server 2008 Standard
  o 1 for the WFE (web front end)
  o 1 for the database server

➤ Twenty (20) Windows Server 2008 CALs

➤ One (1) SQL Server Standard Edition (2005 or 2008)

➤ Twenty (20) Microsoft SQL Server CALs

➤ One (1) SharePoint Server 2010

➤ Twenty (20) SharePoint 2010 CALs, Standard Edition
  o One (1) for each user is required since SharePoint 2010 CALs are additive

➤ Ten (10) SharePoint 2010 2010 CALs, Enterprise Edition
  o One (1) for each user that will be using Enterprise features is required

**Scenario E: SharePoint Server 2010 Intranet and Extranet Site**

Org wants an intranet site for 20 staff using SharePoint Server 2010 and also wants an extranet website. The extranet site could be volunteer sites, a social network site, committee sites, etc.

This is a single environment consisting of both public-facing Internet site and a staff use site for 20 employees. This would be a dual server farm with a web server running SharePoint 2010 and a database server running SQL Server 2008. All 20 employees, all members, and anonymous users will utilize Enterprise features.

➤ Two (2) Windows Server 2008 Standard
  o 1 for the WFE (web front end)
  o 1 for the database server

➤ Twenty (20) Windows Server 2008 CALs

➤ Two (2) Windows Server 2008 External Connector

➤ One (1) SQL Server 2008 Standard Edition, Processor (no CALs required)

➤ One (1) SharePoint Server 2010 for Internet Sites

➤ One (1) SharePoint Server 2010

➤ Twenty (20) SharePoint 2010 CALs, Standard Edition

➤ Twenty (20) SharePoint 2010 CALs, Enterprise Edition

Remember: In addition to the SharePoint Server 2010 for Internet Sites, this environment requires a SharePoint Server 2010 license and appropriate CALs because there are STAFF-ONLY sites running in addition to the other sites.

### Scenario F: Standard Public-facing Small Farm

Org wants a public-facing website using SharePoint Server 2010. This is a two-server configuration with web server running SharePoint Server 2010 Standard, and database server running SQL 2008.

> ➢ Two (2) Windows Server 2008 Standard Edition, 1 web and 1 database server.

> ➢ Two (2) Windows Server 2008 External Connector

> ➢ One (1) SQL Server 2008 Standard Edition – Processor

> ➢ One (1) SharePoint Server 2010 for Internet Sites, Standard

### Scenario G: Enterprise Public-facing Medium Farm

Org wants a public-facing website using SharePoint Server 2010 with Enterprise features. This environment is running on five (5) servers: 2 SQL, 2 SharePoint Web and 1 SharePoint App.

> ➢ Five (5) Windows Server 2008 Standard
>> o 2 for the WFE
>> o 1 for the SharePoint App/Search

- o 2 for the database server

➤ Two (2) Microsoft SQL Server 2008 Standard Processor

➤ Three (3) SharePoint Server 2010 for Internet Sites, Enterprise

➤ Five (5) Windows Server 2008 External Connector Licenses

That's right! All 5 servers require external connectors.

## Scenario H: Enterprise Internet, Intranet, and Extranet Sites

Org with 20 staff wants everything on SharePoint. They want a public-facing website, an intranet, a social network, extranet, and any other site they can ever imagine. They want to be fully licensed for anything they can think of for SharePoint. All 20 employees will utilize Enterprise features. This environment is running on five (5) servers: 2 SQL, 2 SharePoint Web and 1 SharePoint App.

➤ Five (5) Windows Server 2008 Standard
  - o 2 for the WFE
  - o 1 for the SharePoint App/Search
  - o 2 for the database server

➤ Five (5) Windows Server 2008 External Connector Licenses

➤ Two (2) Microsoft SQL Server 2008 Standard Processor

➢ Three (3) SharePoint Server 2010 for Internet Sites, Enterprise

➢ Three (3) Microsoft SharePoint Server 2010

➢ Twenty (20) SharePoint 2010 CALs, Standard

➢ Twenty (20) SharePoint 2010 CALs, Enterprise

Remember that SharePoint CALs are additive so each staff accessing Enterprise features needs both CALs. Also, for an environment with both staff-only and mixed usage, you need to purchase both types of licensing.

## How much does SharePoint cost?

You may find it hard to believe, but everyone asks about costs and fees. SharePoint license costs change frequently and vary by vendor. Each reseller that you talk to will have different prices – definitely shop around. There are also different licensing tiers. If your organization is an eligible charity, then you will get significantly discounted pricing. There are pricing tiers for educational institutes and government agencies. There are different Microsoft pricing tiers depending on how your org purchases. There is Microsoft Open License (with different levels), Microsoft Select, Microsoft Select Plus and many more options. You'll find that many of these license costs are even negotiable.

If you work for a nonprofit, try and make use of TechSoup, located at www.techsoup.org. TechSoup offers nonprofits extremely discounted software, in addition to free information, resources and support.

## Licensing FAQs

We've covered a lot of ground, but there is still much to learn. Here are some SharePoint Licensing FAQs.

**Q: My org has a lot of staff users who will be using SharePoint 2010. Can we just purchase the SharePoint 2010 for Internet Sites license and use that for "staff only" sites?**

A: No. If you will have "private sites" used exclusively by your staff, then this requires SharePoint Server 2010, plus at least the SharePoint 2010 Standard CAL for each employee who will use the Site. If you have 1200 Sites in your SharePoint 2010 environment and just a single Site is 'staff only', then you need to purchase licenses based on CALs for your staff.

**Q: Does every server need SharePoint 2010 installed?**

A: Every SharePoint server in the farm needs a server license, whether WFE, Index, Query, etc. – except for dedicated SQL Servers which are not running any SharePoint services. If the server is running any of the SharePoint services, then you must ensure that the server has the appropriate SharePoint 2010 license. Additionally, each SharePoint server needs the same set of server licenses. For example, if you are running an Internet-facing farm that has two WFE and one index server, you must use the SharePoint 2010 for Internet Sites license on all three servers. If you are running a single three-server farm that is supporting your

Intranet, Extranet, and Internet sites, you must run two different licenses on each of the three servers: SharePoint 2010 for Internet Sites (for public access) and SharePoint Server 2010 (for employees-only sites, for which you would also need appropriate CALs for staff). (Rule is spell out single digit numbers but use numerical for two or greater digit numbers. Ex: One cow was among six brown heifers in the herd of 24 cattle.)

**Q: If we were to initially deploy the "Internet Server" version, would we be able to later launch private sites for users who were covered by individual CALs (staff)?**

A: Yes. The SharePoint 2010 licensing model allows for both versions of the product (internal and external) to be installed on the same farm. If you deploy SharePoint 2010 for Internet Sites only, and then decide you want to add Sites for CAL-based users later, you need to purchase the appropriate CALs and the SharePoint 2010 Server license in addition to the Internet license. The Internet Sites license cannot be used with CALs, because CALs are only usable with the SharePoint 2010 Server license.

**Q: Where do I install a SharePoint 2010 CAL?**

A: You don't install the CALs anywhere. Like a lot of Microsoft software, SharePoint 2010 environments are based upon the 'honor system'. You must have appropriate licensing to utilize the software, but there is no actual licensing check that will disable unlicensed users from accessing your SharePoint 2010 server farm. SharePoint 2010 has usage logging that can be used to determine who is accessing your SharePoint 2010 environment to help keep you licensed correctly.

**Q: We want to deploy an EXTRANET – Sites that will be used for collaboration between Staff and Non-Staff (partners, members, customers, etc...). What license do we need?**

A: Extranets are the one area where there is some licensing flexibility. To be clear, we are defining a SharePoint 2010 Extranet as containing collaborative Sites that are *not* staff-only and do not allow public or anonymous users. Every single user is authenticated. For this type of Site, you have two options.

Option 1: You could purchase the SharePoint Server 2010 license and the appropriate CALs for ALL authenticating users – staff and non-staff.

Option 2: You could purchase the SharePoint Server 2010 for Internet Sites license and no CALs. If you want to run even a single STAFF ONLY site, then you must purchase the SharePoint Server 2010 and CALs.

**Q: If we are deploying Excel Services, Access Services or Visio Services, do we need licenses of Office 2010 for everyone?**

A: Maybe. Users consuming Excel Services do not need to have Excel installed. Same goes for Access Services and Visio Services – consumers do not need Office clients. However, any user wishing to create spreadsheets using Excel to deploy on the Excel Services component of SharePoint 2010 Enterprise will need an Excel 2010 license. If your consultant or contractor is developing all your spreadsheets, then that is the individual who needs Excel 2010 – not your staff.

**Q: I have external users who already have SharePoint 2010 in their own companies (not our org). Can they access our systems with their own licenses, or would we still have to purchase new CALs for them?**

A: You cannot use CALs from an external license for anything in your org.

**Q: Do I need Microsoft Office 2010 to use Microsoft SharePoint Server 2010?**

A: No. In fact, you do not even need to use any version of the Microsoft Office desktop application to get a tremendous amount of benefit from SharePoint 2010.

You can use SharePoint 2010 for content management, surveys, discussion boards, picture Libraries, web pages, email records management, content types, and many other things (including document management for PDFs, PSDs, TIF, GIF, JPG, plus many more non-Office document types) without purchasing or using any version of Microsoft Office.

If you are using the document collaboration features, you can get a lot of benefits from using Microsoft Office. The later the version of Office, the more features you will have access to. You can, however, leverage older versions of Microsoft Office with SharePoint 2010, including Office XP, Office 2003, Office 2007, and Office 2010.

**Q: Can I use FAST Search for SharePoint with SharePoint 2010, Standard, or SharePoint Foundation 2010?**

A: No. FAST Search for SharePoint requires SharePoint Server 2010, Enterprise. For internal use, you simply purchase the FAST Search for SharePoint server license. For external use, there is no different license to purchase. You must purchase an additional license for SharePoint Server 2010 for Internet Sites and Enterprise, and add another server to the farm dedicated to running FAST.

# SharePoint Hosting: Find Your Home

Your SharePoint farm needs to reside somewhere. We're guessing that your org, as a nonprofit or association, does not include hosting SharePoint farms as a core competency. That does not necessarily mean you don't have legitimate reasons to host your farm on-premise. On-premise hosting, or hosting your own farm on your own servers at your own physical location, is just one option. Other options include paying a hosting facility or hosting your SharePoint farm in the cloud in a Software as a Service (SaaS) model.

Each option has unique advantages and disadvantages. We will review the total cost of ownership for each, as well as other important considerations such as uptime and availability, ease of implementation and maintenance, and security. Though some orgs choose a hybrid approach and use a blend of these options, hosting can be divided into three primary categories:

> ➢ On-premise – go it alone

> ➢ Hosted – utilize a hosting facility

> ➢ Software as a Service (SaaS) – use the cloud

## On-Premise Hosting

An on-premise solution means your org provides the server hardware, network, bandwidth, software licenses, and associated infrastructure at *your* location. This includes costs associated with

299

both the initial implementation as well as with the on-going maintenance. Your org is responsible for everything – software, service packs, updates, patches, backups and restores, hardware maintenance, problems, and upgrades.

Your org is also responsible for providing network support personnel. You need someone to manage the servers – Windows, SQL, and SharePoint. You need someone to support the environment day and night. When a server stops responding at 3:00AM, someone needs to fix it.

It may sound a little daunting, but many orgs have been doing this for years. You may consider outsourcing this support, as there are IT firms specializing in these tasks that deliver outstanding service. Some of these firms even provide the hardware, further reducing your direct overhead.

## Performance

The performance of your on-premise SharePoint rests squarely on careful planning and implementation. Make sure you understand the expected load that the solution will be taking on, as well as the availability requirements.

The hardware (physical or virtual) requirements can be accurately calculated if you provide realistic usage estimates. The performance of your SharePoint solution in an on-premise scenario is completely within your control. In order to maintain performance standards, you need to carefully monitor your solution utilization and capacity.

## Uptime/Availability

Service Level Agreements (SLA) of 99.9% uptime are easier said than done, but definitely not impossible. A 99.9% uptime SLA equates to 10 minutes of downtime per week. The infamous five nines (99.999% uptime) SLA is difficult and expensive. The on-premise scenario means you are fully responsible to maintain whatever uptime and availability standards your org demands.

## Ease of Implementation & Maintenance

Of all the hosting options available, on-premise should be considered the most difficult to implement with the greatest degree of ongoing maintenance. This should come as no surprise since on-premise requires that you to do everything. You configure the servers, install SharePoint, and keep it all running smoothly into the future.

It is not difficult to implement a SharePoint solution properly, but it pays to have a clear understanding of the solution and a thoughtfully crafted approach prior to initiation. In fact, the planning of required hardware and software for an on-premise solution is not unlike the planning required for any of the other hosting options. Implementation and maintenance are, however, clearly different.

## Total Cost of Ownership

When calculating the Total Cost of Ownership (TCO), be sure to keep the following line items in mind for on-premise hosting:

- ➢ Software Licensing
    - o Windows Server
    - o SQL Server
    - o SharePoint Server
    - o Backup Agents
    - o Antivirus Agents
    - o Network Monitoring
- ➢ Hardware
    - o SQL Server(s)
    - o SharePoint Server(s)
- ➢ Network Infrastructure (firewall, router, switch, etc.)
- ➢ Power (including UPS)
- ➢ Hardware servicing fees
- ➢ Disaster Preparation Plans (Backups, Offsite storage)
- ➢ Staffing (recurring IT personnel costs, training, documentation)
- ➢ Internet Connectivity (recurring bandwidth costs)
- ➢ Initial Configuration/Setup

## Advantages

The on-premise scenario is by far the most flexible hosting model available. You have complete control of every aspect, including customizations which may not be permitted in other hosting models. Security concerns are a major consideration when choosing to host on-premise – you are in full control of the entire environment, so you have full control of the security model.

## Disadvantages

The Total Cost of Ownership (TCO) is considerably higher than all other options. Your org is responsible for ensuring the uptime and availability. You are responsible for the initial installation, configuration, and ongoing maintenance.

## When to choose on-premise

> ➤ Your org already has a network operations center (NOC). Some larger orgs already have an infrastructure with power, bandwidth, support personnel, backup solutions, antivirus solutions, and various other investments to run and maintain their own environments. Serious consideration should be given before using this as a primary reason "just because that's the way we've always done it."

> ➤ You are confident in your ability to implement and maintain enterprise level solutions (either in-house or outsourced).

> ➤ A security policy prevents you from storing data and/or information outside your internal network. Private clouds may present a valid alternative as well.

# Hosting Facility (Dedicated Servers)

Hosting a SharePoint environment with a third-party hosting facility is a very common hosting option for orgs of all sizes. This is likely due to the many benefits and short-term cost savings this option provides. Many orgs choose the third-party hosting facility option because it allows them to focus more of their time and resources on their mission and objectives.

Most hosting facilities provide 24x7 server-monitoring and support personnel. Backups are typically performed according to industry best practices, and the network backbone and power source typically fail-over to redundant alternatives should the need arise. Utilizing a hosting provider is usually quicker to implement than on-premise hosting because you typically do not have to procure your own hardware.

## Performance

The performance of your SharePoint Farm in a third-party hosting facility also requires careful planning and implementation. While in most cases the hardware setup will be handled by the hosting provider, you still need to do the planning part. Like the on-premise hosting option, you need to understand the expected load (usage) and availability requirements. Your actual hardware requirements can be calculated based upon expected usage.

If all servers are equal, the performance of your SharePoint solution in a hosted environment is likely to be better than your on-premise deployment simply because of the superior infrastructure provided by the third-party hosting company. Hosting facilities will typically have a significantly better network infrastructure in place because this is a core competency of their business – not yours. You still can't overlook planning. Performance planning is just as important with this option as it is with the on-premise option.

## Uptime/Availability

Many hosting facilities offer a Service Level Agreement (SLA) of 99.9% uptime or better. Understand the fine print of the SLA when researching hosting facilities as this is one of the key benefits of choosing this option.

It's a stress reliever knowing that the hosting provider will maintain the uptime and availability standards you have identified.

Finally, demand that your hosting contracts include language pertaining to money backs in the event the hosting provider fails to achieve the contractually agreed-upon SLA.

## Ease of Implementation and Maintenance

Maintenance of your SharePoint environment in a hosted environment is significantly less than the on-premise hosting option. You gain efficiency on the implementation side because your provider will setup the hardware and possibly the Windows Server environments. Your hosting provider will also be responsible for maintaining the hardware and resolving problems, reducing your ongoing maintenance overhead.

## Total Cost of Ownership

When calculating the Total Cost of Ownership (TCO), be sure to keep the following line items in mind for the third-party hosting facility option:

- ➢ Software licensing may be included in the monthly hosting fee or you may provide your own license.
  - o Windows Server
  - o SQL Server
  - o SharePoint Server
- ➢ Hardware will likely be provided. Very few hosting providers allow you to procure your own hardware.
  - o SQL Server(s)
  - o SharePoint Server(s)
  - o Active Directory Server(s). If implementing an Intranet solution that requires authentication from your existing domain, you may elect to use an offsite AD server, ADFS, LDAP, or another solution. Determine all costs involved from configuration to ongoing maintenance.
- ➢ Network Infrastructure (firewall, router, switch, etc.). Firewalls are sometimes included in the monthly hosting fees but may incur additional costs.
- ➢ Power including UPS
- ➢ Hardware servicing fees. Determine what costs are associated if hardware fails and needs to be replaced.
- ➢ Disaster Preparation Plans like backups and offsite storage are typically included in the monthly fees.

Validate backup retention periods, restoration processes, and time estimates. Do not just assume that the backup and restoral process will meet the needs of your org. Validate every aspect.

➤ Staffing and Help Desk are typically included.

➤ Internet Connectivity is typically included. Many hosting facilities will provide a certain amount of bandwidth as part of the base monthly fee and your org will pay additional fees for additional bandwidth utilized.

➤ Initial Configuration/Setup is usually a one-time fee.

## Advantages

Third-party hosting solutions provide many of the same benefits as on-premise deployments. Your org maintains control of the environment even though it's not physically hosted at your facility. The initial cost is typically lower than when using a hosting provider because you typically do not have to purchase the hardware. The infrastructure is generally more powerful than an on-premise deployment resulting in greater performance, availability, and stability (though not always – test this!).

Long term costs will be lower than on-premise when factoring in the staff, training, equipment, software, and maintenance required. This option is usually more secure than an on-premise deployment as most hosting providers have staff dedicated to security. Many orgs have staff that must be jack-or-jill-of-all-trades responsible for server configuration, networking, firewalls, patches, updates, help desk, and many more.

It is much easier to plan a budget for a hosted deployment. Monthly costs are fixed. This option also provides the same flexibility as on-premise with regard to SharePoint customizations and configurations. This is your dedicated environment; you still have control.

## Disadvantages

Recurring monthly costs can seem expensive if you are only comparing hardware and software costs. You must account for *all variables* for an accurate comparison.

You may also see discrepancies in hardware costs because you are not dealing with the hardware vendor directly. We have seen the cost of adding memory (like RAM) be upwards of 500% more than ordering directly online! Negotiate!

### When to choose dedicated hosting

> ➤ Performance and availability are extremely important.

> ➤ Your budget can support the recurring monthly costs.

> ➤ You do not have a prohibitive security policy forcing you to maintain data on-premise.

> ➤ If your solution requires heavy customizations you have two hosting options: on-premise and dedicated hosting. Choose dedicated hosting if you need heavy customizations but don't want the burden of on-premise hosting.

# Cloud Hosting (SaaS)

Software as a Service (SaaS) or the "cloud" is just a shared environment. Hosting your SharePoint solution *in the cloud* means you are renting everything: hardware, software, bandwidth, and support personnel.

The cost is low because you are sharing resources with many others doing the same thing. This model has been gaining popularity for years, partly because the limitations once associated with shared environments are diminishing thanks to better application architectures. In fact, SharePoint 2010 was architected from the ground up with an inherent multi-tenant (shared) architecture.

The main reason the SaaS hosting model is growing exponentially is because it's just so affordable! You get many of the same benefits of a dedicated hosted environment (key word there was "many", not "all"), and it has the lowest cost of entry and TCO of all options.

## Performance

SharePoint in the cloud can often outperform on-premise SharePoint deployments. The infrastructure used in cloud computing is often more capable, more stable, and more reliable than any other solution. The larger SaaS providers also include failover architectures that may not otherwise be affordable in the on-premise or dedicated hosted solutions.

## Uptime/Availability

Hosting your SharePoint solution in the cloud may be the best way to ensure uptime and availability. Not unlike the dedicated hosting option, cloud hosting providers offer a Service Level Agreement (SLA) of 99.9% uptime. You should ensure this is in fact the case when researching cloud hosting providers. Read the fine print of all agreements!

## Ease of Implementation and Maintenance

Implementation does not get any easier than with SharePoint in the cloud. Ongoing maintenance is also easy. You do not have to do anything at all; your cloud provider handles everything from OS updates and patches, to application service packs and hotfixes.

## Total Cost of Ownership

Cloud hosting is likely to be the most cost effective solution you research. When calculating the Total Cost of Ownership (TCO), be sure to keep the following line items in mind for the cloud or SaaS option:

- Software licensing will be included in the monthly hosting fee.
  - Windows Server
  - SQL Server
  - SharePoint Server
- Hardware will be included in the monthly hosting fee.
  - SQL Server(s)
  - SharePoint Server(s)

- o Active Directory Server(s). If implementing an Intranet solution which requires authentication from your existing domain, you may elect to use your existing AD. Determine all costs involved from configuration to ongoing maintenance.
- ➤ Network Infrastructure will be included in the monthly hosting fee.
- ➤ Power will be included in the monthly hosting fee.
- ➤ Hardware servicing fees will be included in the monthly hosting fee.
- ➤ Disaster Preparation Plans will be included in the monthly hosting fee.
- ➤ Staffing and help desk will be included in the monthly hosting fee.
- ➤ Internet Connectivity will be included in the monthly hosting fee. Some cloud providers will allow a specific amount of bandwidth as part of the base monthly fee, and your org will pay additional fees for additional bandwidth utilized.
- ➤ Initial Configuration/Setup is usually a one-time fee.

## Advantages

The value proposition is the major benefit to hosting your SharePoint solution in the cloud. You will save a lot of money in both the short-term and long-term. Performance and availability are also fantastic benefits of the cloud. The initial cost of entry is the lowest of all hosting options.

## Disadvantages

So what's the catch?  In a word, the catch to hosting SharePoint in the cloud amounts to customization.  Since the very nature of cloud computing is about shared resources, customizations are tricky.  The SharePoint 2010 multi-tenant model (used in cloud) allows some customizations – but not all.

You will only be able to take your SharePoint solution so far until you hit this boundary.  To be very clear, your ability to use third-party Web Parts or deploy custom features will be severely limited in a cloud-based environment.  This is changing daily and will improve through time.

## When to choose cloud (SaaS) hosting

> ➤ You want high-end performance and availability.

> ➤ Your org can get by without customizations.

> ➤ You want your environment configured immediately.

> ➤ You want to use your budget for out-of-the-box configuration and training.

## SharePoint Farm:  Small, Medium, or Large?

SharePoint Farm topologies come in three sizes:  small, medium, and large.  The size of your org and how you are using SharePoint will influence your SharePoint Farm topology.  The topology is also influenced by the number of actual users, the amount of content, the type of content, and the level of collaboration you expect.  You need to understand the number of users who will have access to the solution, and what those users will be doing.  Microsoft has published guidelines for SharePoint Farm planning:

➤ Small farms are typically adequate for solutions serving fewer than 50,000 users.

➤ Medium farms typically work out for solutions serving fewer than 100,000 users.

➤ Large farms typically handle solutions serving fewer than 500,000 users.

➤ If your solution needs to serve more than 500,000 users, then you will still use a large farm topology but will likely need to join multiple farms together.

## Capacity Planning

There are two types of capacity that you need to account for: storage capacity and usage capacity.

### Storage Capacity Planning

Microsoft provides storage capacity planning worksheets to assist with capacity planning, but you need to evaluate the type of content that you will be storing in SharePoint. What content are you migrating into SharePoint? Are you using Versioning? Are you promoting collaboration? Storage capacity planning is important for the long-term health of your SharePoint environment.

For storage capacity planning considerations, you can also follow this general rule to help determine the amount of storage required for near-term future growth:

> ➤ Plan for 200% of the total size of all documents currently stored in your file share or content database.

> ➤ Plan an additional 50% of the total size (above) for your Index (used by Search).

## Usage Capacity Planning

For usage capacity planning considerations, you can also follow this general rule to help determine farm topology size: Plan for one request per second per one thousand users (1 RPS/1000 users).

➢ Small farms can typically serve 100 requests per second.

➢ Medium farms can typically serve 200 requests per second.

While these guidelines are helpful, you still need to determine if your users will be mostly consuming content (which is not resource intensive) or if they will be generating charts and graphs on dashboard pages, aggregating a lot of content and utilizing Excel/Access/PerformancePoint Services (very resource intensive).

The key to effective usage capacity planning is to think in terms of *most users* rather than *some users*. Plan for the majority of users. Many SharePoint solutions end up including dashboard pages to serve a handful of users who do not represent the majority. These users should be considered but should not heavily influence your sizing decisions. Identify the types of activities the majority will be doing and be sure to use this as a primary factor in determining your SharePoint farm topology size, hardware selection, and hosting configuration.

# Hosting Option Sheet

Hosting Option: _____

*(fill out this sheet for every option)*

| Deployment timeline | |
|---|---|
| Reliability (1-5) 5 is best | 1  2  3  4  5 |
| Ease of implementation (1-5) 5 is best | 1  2  3  4  5 |
| Uptime/Availability (SLA) | |

Hardware
- Servers                              $_____
- Bandwidth                         $_____
- Network Hardware             $_____
- UPS Backup                        $_____

Licensing
- Windows Server                 $_____
- Windows External Connector   $_____
- SharePoint Server              $_____
- SharePoint CALs                 $_____
- SQL Server                         $_____

Support
- Staff                                    $_____
- Depreciation                      $_____
- Initial Setup                       $_____

Maintenance costs
- Backups/Restores               $_____
- Security                              $_____
- Antivirus                             $_____
- System Monitoring             $_____
- Application Monitoring      $_____
- Problem Resolution           $_____

Total Setup         $_____
Total Monthly         $_____
Total Annual (yr 1)         $_____
Total Annual (yr 2)         $_____
Total Annual (yr 3)         $_____
Total Cost of Ownership (TCO)         $_____

## Summary

You have more SharePoint hosting options today than ever before. Each option has **advantages** and **disadvantages**, though hosting in the cloud is becoming more attractive every day.

Make time to carefully understand the pros and cons of your hosting options, and you will be in a great position to make this very important decision.

Hosting options include **on-premise, dedicated** hosting solutions, and **cloud** hosting (**SaaS**).

Carefully consider **performance, uptime** and **availability**, ease of **implementation, maintenance**, total cost of ownership (**TCO**), SharePoint farm **size, storage** capacity planning, and **usage** capacity planning for each hosting option.

# Is SharePoint a good fit?

Hopefully you've learned a lot about SharePoint. You know about a lot of different features and functions. You've learned about different versions, hosting options, example solutions, and how orgs everywhere are leveraging SharePoint today.

Perhaps you have also heard some scary things about SharePoint. We've heard them, too. We've heard horror stories of SharePoint going awry. We've heard anti-Microsoft and even anti-SharePoint propaganda time and time again. We have seen SharePoint ignored by orgs when they should have at least considered it.

We've heard so many reasons why you should not consider SharePoint we had to include a few of our favorites.

## Our org is just too small for SharePoint

This is a real possibility. You might be a one person shop. You don't collaborate with anyone. You are happy to keep all of your organizational knowledge on your laptop. You use Wordpress for your public-facing website. You don't need a business platform. You don't need a platform at all. You have no committees, councils, chapters, boards, special interest groups or teams. How could you? It's just you.

However, if you have at least two people, then you might consider SharePoint. We would recommend looking at a hosted or SaaS model for a smaller team.

A small org should not be spending time managing servers and installing software. A small org should pay an affordable monthly rate and get enterprise level support.

The two-person team of authors of this very book used SharePoint to manage creating and editing this very content. Why? SharePoint gave us version control, exclusive editing rights, task assignments, a shared calendar, alert notifications, simultaneous document authoring when we needed it, and was available via web access.

If one of us had 15 minutes sitting at the airport, we could open a chapter and write a little. We never had to wonder if the document had been modified. We never had to wonder who had the latest version.

## SharePoint is too complicated for our org

SharePoint can be complicated. It *can* be very complicated. It's a large platform with a lot of capabilities. This sophistication can sometimes be overwhelming. But SharePoint can also be simple.

Simplify your experience by simplifying SharePoint. Simplify SharePoint by hiding or disabling templates, features, and services which are not needed. Not only will this improve the performance of your SharePoint environment, but it will also make user training and adoption easier.

SharePoint can be intimidating due to the many capabilities, options, and menus. Provide proper training to your users. Things may seem complicated right up to the moment you understand them.

## SharePoint isn't Designer Friendly

Way back in 2001 and even in 2003, SharePoint was not designer friendly. SharePoint was originally built for businesses to use for internal collaboration with Internet Explorer. That was a long time ago, and SharePoint has had to live with that albatross ever since.

To be effective with SharePoint, a designer does need to learn a little about how to style SharePoint. They need to understand SharePoint templates. Specifically, they need to learn how Master Pages and Page Layouts work together to style SharePoint.

SharePoint does use standards for styling. It's the same HTML and CSS standards that are used everywhere.

## We don't even know where to start with SharePoint

Congratulations! You have found where to start. By investing the time to read this book, you are well on your way. You've already made the wise decision to read this book.

We give presentations, teach classes, and speak at numerous SharePoint events. We work with experts and with people who have never seen SharePoint. The best way for you to start using SharePoint is to **start using SharePoint**. That's it.

People learn better by doing. You can read a book, watch a video, see a presentation, but you need to jump in and use it. You will be using SharePoint to do REAL WORK within minutes without training.

When you browse to a SharePoint team Site, there are a couple of links that jump out. Shared Documents are pretty self-explanatory. Calendar needs very little overview. You'll be able to create an Event with two clicks.

You should still get training, you should still read books, and you should still go to user group meetings. Your org should put forth careful consideration and use strategies like those outlined in this book to implement SharePoint as a strategic business platform. However, you should not be afraid to use SharePoint.

## SharePoint is too expensive.

Really? SharePoint can be extremely cost-effective. If you already have a Windows Server, then SharePoint Foundation is free (see the chapter on Licensing for full details). We are not trying to mislead anyone with this statement. SharePoint is only free with Windows Server.

While pretty significant in capability, SharePoint Foundation does not provide all of the functionality of SharePoint 2010 Standard or SharePoint 2010 Enterprise (neither of which are free).

When evaluating the ROI of utilizing any business platform, consider the sheer breadth of capability, the ecosystem of support providers, and the number of free resources like blogs, user groups, and conferences. Suddenly SharePoint looks much more affordable.

## We tried SharePoint already, and it was a disaster.

We have seen SharePoint implemented poorly. When poorly implemented, SharePoint can be a complete disaster within an org. We have been called in to rescue SharePoint projects and even been told, "We need help, but please don't use the word SharePoint. That's a bad word here!"

Why did SharePoint fail?

- ➢ Poor planning

- ➢ Unclear goals and objectives

- ➢ Objectives changed during the project

- ➢ Unrealistic time or resource estimates

- ➢ Lack of executive support and user involvement

- ➢ Failure to communicate and act as a team

- ➢ Inappropriate skills

Poor SharePoint implementations occur for a variety of reasons. Like many less-than-stellar technology implementations, failed SharePoint projects can usually be traced back to poor planning and a lack of understanding of the technology.

## SharePoint has performance issues

We agree. While improvements have been made, we still feel Microsoft has plenty of room for improving the performance of the SharePoint platform.

To avoid potential performance related issues, be sure to plan your farm topology accordingly to your expected usage.

For larger environments, there are some great third-party utilities which are specifically designed to optimize and enhance SharePoint performance.

## SharePoint isn't a *Real* CMS

With SharePoint 2007, Microsoft merged Content Management Server (MCMS) into SharePoint to create sophisticated capabilities for using SharePoint as a Web Content Management (WCM) solution. With SharePoint 2010, the WCM features are enhanced again.

So how do we determine whether SharePoint is a real WCM or not? It's clearly running thousands of websites effectively, so we went straight to the definitive guide to all human knowledge. Wikipedia.

Wikipedia lists the following components of modern web content management systems in **bold**. SharePoint may not provide every niche gadget or widget, but we think you'll agree that SharePoint provides robust capabilities as a CMS.

**Automated templates.** Create standard output templates which can be automatically applied to new and existing content, allowing the appearance of all content to be changed from one central place.

Through the use of Master Pages, Page Layouts, and Themes, SharePoint allows you to customize your entire Site's look and feel, including Page level customizations using Page Layouts and Web Parts.

**Scalable expansion.** Available in most modern WCMSs is the ability to expand a single implementation (one installation on one server) across multiple domains.

SharePoint can run multiple Sites using multiple URLs on a single server install. SharePoint is scalable and can run as a standalone server or a multi-server farm.

**Easily editable content.** Once content is separated from the visual presentation of a site, it usually becomes much easier and quicker to edit and manipulate. Most WCMS software includes WYSIWYG editing tools allowing non-technical individuals to create and edit content.

This is best illustrated using a screen capture of a vanilla SharePoint page in edit mode. Notice the page editing toolbar (Ribbon) has an uncanny resemblance to Microsoft Word.

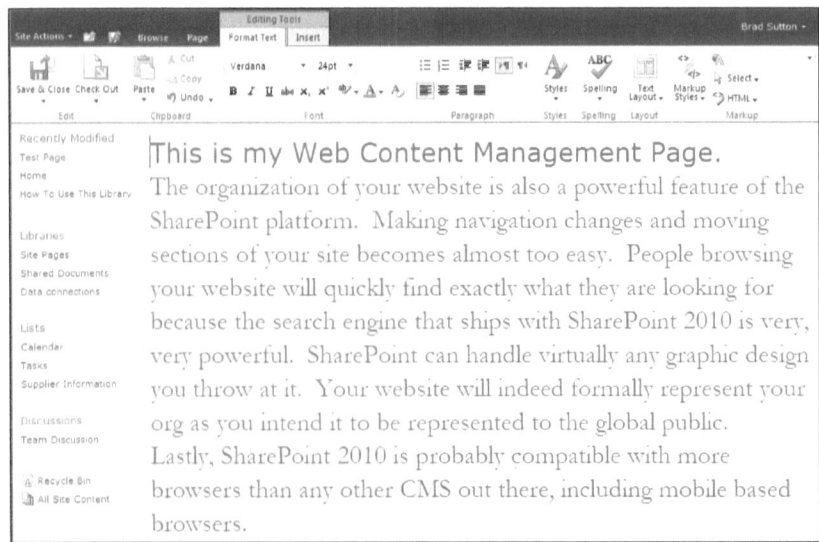

**SharePoint WYSIWYG Editor**

**Scalable feature sets. Most WCMS software includes plug-ins or modules that can be easily installed to extend an existing site's functionality.**

It's arguable that there isn't a single platform anywhere that has more plug-ins, modules, Web Parts, features, samples, templates, and global support than SharePoint. You can extend the platform to perform thousands of tasks and integrate seamlessly into hundreds of existing systems – much of it without writing any code.

SharePoint has a framework for installing add-ons called Features that makes it easy to activate and deactivate add-ons at the Site Collection or Site level for complete control.

**Web standards upgrades.** Active WCMS software usually receives regular updates that include new feature sets and keep the system up to current web standards.

SharePoint 2010 is in the fourth major version of SharePoint. In addition to the innovation that Microsoft continuously adds, SharePoint has the support of an entire global ecosystem available. It would be hard to find another platform with a faster rate of innovation.

**Workflow management.** Workflow is the process of creating cycles of sequential and parallel tasks that must be accomplished in the CMS. For example, a content creator can submit a story, but it is not published until the copy editor cleans it up and the editor-in-chief approves it.

Workflow. It's in there. You can configure three-state approval Workflows, make your own publishing approvals, associate Workflows with Content Types, send emails, update information/data, and much more.

**Delegation.** Some CMS software allows for various user groups to have limited privileges over specific content on the website, spreading out the responsibility of content management.

Security. SharePoint provides very granular security capabilities.

**Document management.** CMS software may provide a means of managing the life cycle of a document from initial creation time, through revisions, publication, archive, and document destruction.

SharePoint has document management with Versioning, exclusive Check Out, Security, publication, Workflow, and automated document retention and archival capabilities.

**Content virtualization. CMS software may provide a means of allowing each user to work within a virtual copy of the entire Web site, document set, and/or code base. This enables changes to multiple interdependent resources to be viewed and/or executed in-context prior to submission.**

Versioning provides authorized content manager the ability to preview, publish, and roll-back content of Pages, wiki entries, blog posts, documents, or any other type of content stored in SharePoint.

We think the idea of each user having an entire copy of the website virtualized is a bit dated – not sure why anyone would need that for anything other than working offline. Offline functionality is accommodated using SharePoint Workspace 2010.

**Content syndication. CMS software often assists in content distribution by generating RSS and Atom data feeds to other systems. They may also e-mail users when updates are available as part of the workflow process.**

With RSS syndication and Alerts natively available on all content and search results, content syndication is inherent in the SharePoint platform.

**Multilingual. Ability to display content in multiple languages.**

SharePoint not only allows you to publish content in nearly any language, it has native AUTHOR and EDITOR support for more than 40 languages.

## SharePoint was written for Developers

The fact is, we couldn't agree more. SharePoint *is* written for developers. One of the benefits of the SharePoint platform is extensibility. The ability to enhance and customize is inherent in every aspect of SharePoint. Your org can make SharePoint *exactly* what you need it to be.

This is a good thing. Unfortunately, this statement is sometimes used to imply SharePoint is complicated. Refer to *SharePoint is too complicated.*

## SharePoint was *not* written for Developers

We sometimes hear this from open source loyalists. You might hear this from developers who are not .NET developers. Perhaps they're experts in a different technology platform like PHP, ColdFusion, or something other than .NET. Consider this: if you ask a PHP developer what the next play should be, the answer will undoubtedly include writing PHP code.

Regardless of where you might have heard it, understand that SharePoint is in fact highly extensible, but you do need the right education and skills.

There are hundreds of vendors selling SharePoint add-ons, features, and components. The rate of innovation is breathtaking. This simply would not be the case if the platform was not easily extensible.

## Summary

Many factors play into determining if SharePoint is a good fit for your org. It is possible that SharePoint is not the right answer. While this chapter addresses some of the things we commonly hear when helping orgs, this entire book aims to help you answer this question.

To determine if SharePoint is a good fit, you need to **clearly identify your org's short- and long-term objectives**, and then support those objectives with **business requirements**.

**Map your business requirements** to out-of-the-box SharePoint functionality. **Analyze** which requirements are satisfied by native SharePoint functionality and which are not.

Finally, **determine the level of effort** involved to satisfy the remaining requirements via SharePoint customizations. Determine if the remaining requirements should leverage configuration, third-party add-ons, or custom development – in that order!

Lastly, and perhaps most importantly, ask questions. **Get educated**. Leverage the SharePoint community. The SharePoint community is unrivaled when it comes to the total number of people that are helpful, friendly, passionate, and excited about SharePoint.

Don't think twice about posting a question to a discussion forum or blog. Go to training, conferences, sessions, and user group meetings. A lot of these are even free. You can also email us.

# Orgs using SharePoint

Thousands of orgs are currently using SharePoint for intranet sites, member communities, extranets, and public-facing websites. Many of these orgs are maximizing their SharePoint investment by utilizing this platform for more than one of these initiatives.

Listing every org using SharePoint is outside the scope of this book. To the best of our knowledge, the following is a list of orgs reportedly using Microsoft SharePoint in some capacity. This list was compiled using public web resources including blogs, published case studies, TopSharePoint.com, and Microsoft.com. The most comprehensive list *we* found was TopSharePoint.com.

- 92nd St Y
- Accueil
- AgStar Financial Services
- Alberta Primary Care Initiative
- Alberta Teachers' Association
- American Academy of Pediatrics
- American Association for the Study of Liver Diseases
- American Association of Advertising Agencies
- American Association of Blood Banks
- American Association of Colleges of Osteopathic Medicine
- American Association of Colleges of Pharmacy
- American Association of Community Colleges
- American Cancer Society

- American College of Allergy, Asthma and Immunology
- American College of Physicians
- American Council for Technology (ACT) – Industry Advisory Council (IAC)
- American Council of Life Insurers
- American Health Care Association
- American Heart Association
- American Industrial Hygiene Association
- American Institute of Aeronautics and Astronautics
- American Institute of Architects
- American Institute of Certified Public Accountants
- American Society of Association Executives
- American Society of Interior Designers
- Associated Students Program Board
- Association for Cancer Research
- Association for the Advancement of Retired Persons
- Association of Flemish Cities and Municipalities
- Association of Performing Arts Presenters
- Association of the United States Army
- Baylor Health Care System
- Bluetooth Special Interest Group
- Cable & Telecommunications Association for Marketing
- Canadian Association of Petroleum Producers

- ➢ Canadian Patient Safety Institute
- ➢ Carnegie Hall
- ➢ Catholic Diocese of Christchurch
- ➢ CFA Institute
- ➢ Chemonics International
- ➢ CHF International
- ➢ Chicago Convention & Tourism Bureau
- ➢ Chicagoland Chamber of Commerce
- ➢ Children International
- ➢ Christian Children's Fund
- ➢ Christian Homes
- ➢ Clearpoint Financial Counseling
- ➢ Cleveland Clinic
- ➢ CMR Institute
- ➢ Community Associations Institute
- ➢ Conservation International
- ➢ Conservation International
- ➢ Costa Brava Girona Tourism Board
- ➢ Council of Landscape Architectural Registration Boards
- ➢ Critical Ecosystem Partnership Fund
- ➢ Cystic Fibrosis Foundation
- ➢ Danish Chamber of Commerce
- ➢ Danish Insurance Association

- ➤ ECRI Institute
- ➤ Edison Electric Institute
- ➤ Environment, Energy, and Sustainability Symposium and Exhibition
- ➤ European Society for Therapeutic Radiology and Oncology
- ➤ Fédération Internationale de l'Automobile
- ➤ FIA Foundation
- ➤ Four Seasons Hospice & Palliative Care
- ➤ GreenStone Farm Credit Services
- ➤ Group Cares
- ➤ Heart Failure Association of the European Society of Cardiology
- ➤ Help for Heroes
- ➤ Home Group
- ➤ Hospice of Northwest Ohio
- ➤ Human Rights Watch
- ➤ Innovation Center for U.S. Dairy
- ➤ Intermountain Healthcare
- ➤ International AIDS Vaccine Initiative
- ➤ International Air Transport Association
- ➤ International Car Wash Association
- ➤ International Code Council
- ➤ International Investors Association of Turkey

- International Monetary Fund
- International Project Management Association
- Kalliolan Setlementti
- Library of Congress
- Make Roads Safe
- Mental Health Commission of Canada
- Motability Operations
- National Apartment Association
- National Association of College and University Business Officers
- National Association of Convenience Stores
- National Association of Tax Professionals
- National Business Travel Association
- National Colorectal Cancer Roundtable
- National Concrete Masonry Association
- National Rural Electric Cooperative Association
- New Zealand Automobile Association
- Noblis
- Northwest Education Loan Association
- Ohio State Bar Association
- Ohio State University Alumni Association
- Ontario Hospital Association
- Oregon Research Institute

- Pennsylvania Patient Safety Authority
- PKW Australia
- Praxity
- Project Management Institute
- Project Scotland
- Promotional Products Association International
- Prospera
- Providence Health & Services
- Psychologist Association
- Resources for the Future
- Right To Play
- Risk and Insurance Management Society
- Royal Yachting Association
- SABO
- Samaritan Health Services
- Shasta Head Start
- Sheet Metal Workers International Association
- Smithsonian Institution
- Society of Critical Care Medicine
- Society of Human Resources Management
- SOS Children's Villages
- Southern York County Business Association
- Special Coffee Association of America

- SSM Cardinal Glennon Children's Medical Center
- St. John Ambulance
- St. Mary's Good Samaritan, Incorporated
- Supporting Kidds
- Swedish Red Cross
- TechSoup.org
- Texas Computer Education Association
- The American Institute of Architects
- The Gideons International
- United Way
- Urban Farming
- Urban Land Institute
- Virginia Farm Bureau
- Voka Alliance
- YKI, Institute for Surface Chemistry

# Index

www.ingramcontent.com/pod-product-compliance
Lightning Source LLC
Chambersburg PA
CBHW020725180526

45163CB00001B/110